HORIZON

WINTER, 1969 · VOLUME XI, NUMBER 1

The Legs of Icarus

The editors of Horizon habitually regard this magazine as a newcomer to the field of journalism, and we are therefore astonished to announce that the volume number on the spine of this issue has turned to XI. Our first issue, published ten years ago, had as its frontispiece Pieter Bruegel's painting of a caravel, which we took as our colophon. The caravel is actually a detail from Bruegel's big, panoramic picture called *The Fall of Icarus*—a curious painting because all you see of Icarus is a pair of legs disappearing into the water. In taking our detail of the painting we omitted Icarus's legs, perhaps because they seemed irrelevant to the image of a splendid voyage just beginning, but perhaps also because they seemed too graphic a symbol of a brave flight ending. Now that we have been airborne for ten years, we feel safe in reproducing the caravel again, this time including the part of the painting that shows Icarus's legs just below the sterncastle of the ship.

In that first issue we were setting out on a voyage to the past, studying man's many cultures for their own sake but always with an eye to the light they can shed on our own modern, Western civilization. C. V. Wedgwood, describing in that issue the rise of the Dutch Republic, showed how adversity can stimulate a society, as it can a man, to its highest peak of achievement. H. R. Trevor-Roper, writing at a time when the Cold War was the dominant reality in foreign affairs, drew an implicit parallel for the twentieth century in "A Case of Coexistence: Christendom and the Turks."

Learning lessons from history is, to be sure, a treacherous game. For history often provides ambiguous answers. From World War II, for instance, we learned the lesson that the nation with the most military hardware always wins the war, and so we sent our army into the jungles of Vietnam armed as if for World War III, against an enemy that fights with other weapons and reads another rule book. We might have avoided the mistake if we, or someone in the Pentagon, had better understood the nature of guerrilla warfare, as expounded in the article by Correlli Barnett beginning on page 4 of this issue.

Yet, what are we to conclude now from Lacey Baldwin Smith's article on the Wars of the Roses? Does his tale of gang war, cruel assassinations, and indiscriminate violence reassure us that our own society cannot be *that* bad? Or are we to agree

AMERICAN HERITAGE PUBLISHING CO.

PRESIDENT
James Parton

EDITORIAL COMMITTEE
Joseph J. Thorndike, *Chairman*
Oliver Jensen
Richard M. Ketchum

SENIOR ART DIRECTOR
Irwin Glusker

SENIOR EDITOR, HORIZON
Marshall B. Davidson

PUBLISHER, HORIZON
Paul Gottlieb

EDITOR
Joseph J. Thorndike
MANAGING EDITOR: Charles L. Mee, Jr.
ARTICLES EDITOR: Robert Cowley   ART EDITOR: Jane Wilson
ART DIRECTOR: Kenneth Munowitz
ASSOCIATE EDITORS: Shirley Tomkievicz, Barbara Klaw, Nancy Kelly
CONTRIBUTING EDITOR: Walter Karp
ASSISTANT EDITORS: Priscilla Flood, Charles Folds
COPY EDITOR: Mary Ann Pfeiffer   *Assistant:* Carol R. Angell

ADVISORY BOARD: Gilbert Highet, *Chairman*, Frederick Burkhardt,
William Harlan Hale, John Walker
EUROPEAN CONSULTING EDITOR: J. H. Plumb, *Christ's College, Cambridge*
EUROPEAN BUREAU: Gertrudis Feliu, *Chief, 11 rue du Bouloi, Paris Ier*

Horizon
A Magazine of the Arts

WINTER, 1969 · VOLUME XI, NUMBER 1

with Anthony Burgess that we are living up to the worst hopes of the Marquis de Sade?

Not all of our questions are so somber, of course. Our little collection of articles about Things (the anthropomorphic pack rat, the Collyer brothers, the potlatch, garbage—and, yes, we have even managed to drag Karl Marx into all this) raises a less sinister question: shall we, or shall we not, live in an oppressive Thingdom?

Of course there is a somber side to that, too. In our next issue Peter Farb, the author of a new book called *Man's Rise to Civilization as Shown by the Indians of North America from Primeval Times to the Coming of the Industrial State*, will consider the subject of messianic cults, viewed as a reaction on the part of those who are not in on the big Thing bonanza.

What shall we make of our troubled time? Is it the dawn of another Renaissance—or the stormy passing of a civilization's peak? We cannot know. But we shall keep asking the questions, if not to answer them, then at least to explore them in the light of the past—all the questions that seem to us to have more than a passing relevance to our present and hoped-for future. For it does seem to us that these are the most rewarding, ultimately the most urgent, questions. Indeed—dare we admit it?—we think they are the most fun to explore.   THE EDITORS

HORIZON is published every three months by American Heritage Publishing Co., Inc. Editorial and executive offices: 551 Fifth Avenue, New York, N.Y. 10017. Treasurer: George W. Breitkreuz. Secretary: John C. Taylor III. All correspondence about subscriptions should be addressed to: HORIZON Subscription Office, 379 West Center St., Marion, Ohio 43302.

Single Copies: $5.00; Subscriptions: $16.00 per year in the U.S. & Canada; elsewhere, $17.00

Annual indexes for Volumes I–IX are available at $1 each. A cumulative index for Volumes I–V is available at $3. HORIZON is also indexed in the *Readers Guide to Periodical Literature*. The editors welcome contributions but can assume no responsibility for unsolicited material. Title registered U.S. Patent Office. Second class postage paid at New York, N.Y., and at additional mailing offices.

COVER: This young woman with the downcast eyes appears in Vermeer's *An Artist in his Studio*. She is posing for an artist who is painting an allegorical work in which she represents, perhaps, the Muse of history. Yet she is also, quite clearly, an ordinary girl dressed up with a few artist's props, which may be Vermeer's own wry allegorical comment upon allegorical art. The riddle of Vermeer and his masterpiece, which is in the collection of the Kunsthistorisches Museum in Vienna, is analyzed in an article beginning on page 94.

CATHERINE LEROY—BLACK STAR; COURTESY *Life* MAGAZINE

North Vietnamese guerrillas await a Marine attack, Hué, 1968

Guerrilla Warfare

The first "guerrillas" ambush Napoleonic troops, Spain, 1811

Since 1949 guerrilla warfare has turned one first-class French army out of Indochina and another out of Algeria; it has turned the British out of Cyprus and the Batista regime out of Cuba; it has held to a draw in Vietnam the most massive industrialized military machine in history. It has been narrowly beaten, after prolonged fighting and expense, and only against enormous odds, in Greece, Malaya, and the Philippines. This record makes a marked contrast to the positive achievements of "conventional" and nuclear war during the same period.

It cannot be too often repeated that just as war is a continuation of policy, the methods and organization of warmaking are a projection of a society in a given country at a given time. In two world wars the advanced industrial nations of the West have consequently made war with elaborate

*How it works
in Southeast Asia, how
it will work
in Latin America,
how it may work
in America's cities,
and why West Point
generals and
police commissioners
can't stop it*

By CORRELLI BARNETT

technical apparatus. Indeed, in the final analysis the two world wars were nothing more than a prolonged and expensive audit to prove that the industrial resources of one side were smaller than those of the other. The West has become increasingly unable to think of combat effectiveness except in terms of ever greater firepower, air power, and mechanization, ever more expensive and sophisticated gadgetry.

We are like a family that believes that a picnic necessarily involves a tent, collapsible tables and chairs, a portable refrigerator, a portable stove, a transistor radio (or television), a chic and lavish meal (most of it prepre-pared in a plant)—and, of course, a large automobile. Perhaps even a light aircraft. And in military terms this kind of elaboration constitutes only what the strategic theorists call "conventional" warfare. Nuclear war is of course industrialized war—gadgetry and firepower—carried to its ultimate. The campus theorists with square foreheads who chop logic about "escalation" and "counterforce" and "counter-city" nuclear strategies, and the defense departments that demand increasingly elaborate antidoomsday warning systems, tend to obscure the basic fact about nuclear weapons: they are unusable except in a suicide pact.

Even "conventional" technological war is a clumsy, expensive, and immensely destructive instrument of policy. Its immense destructiveness has made war unthinkable as a deliberate means of realizing political aims. Technology has led war up a dead end.

And yet it was in 1949, the year Russia exploded its first atomic bomb and ushered in the nuclear stalemate, that under an entirely different conception of war the Chinese Communists completed the most astonishing and history-changing victory of modern times by wresting China from Chiang Kai-shek and the Nationalists. The victory was accomplished after some twenty years of struggle by an army that grew from a handful of guerrillas armed with ancient or homemade weapons. It was the first and greatest success of what Mao Tse-tung, the Chinese Communist leader and theorist, calls "revolutionary war." Revolutionary war grows out of traditional guerrilla war. It pulls the rug from under the Western belief that mechanized firepower and large industrial resources are the only keys to victory in the twentieth century.

"...Mao Tse-tung and disciples such as General Vo Nguyen Giap... have noted the weaknesses of an enemy who dislikes getting out of his car and who divorces military affairs from politics."

A distinction must be made straightaway between guerrilla war and revolutionary war. Guerrilla war—murder, assassination, sabotage, and ambush—is an ancient method of doing damage to armies that you are not strong enough to take on in pitched battle. The crucial contribution of the Asian Communists has been to place guerrilla warfare within a political framework and employ it for political purposes. The framework is political indoctrination of the people, coupled with social reform; the purpose is revolution, the toppling of an existing regime by violence. However, the Communists have transformed the traditional conception of guerrilla warfare even within the purely military sphere. No longer is it a secondary military activity, an adjunct to the decisive operations of a conventional army. In Communist theory and practice guerrilla warfare becomes itself the means of decision, and Mao Tse-tung and disciples such as General Vo Nguyen Giap have dignified it with its own theory and strategic and tactical doctrine. They have examined the geographical and social prerequisites; they have noted the weaknesses of an enemy who dislikes getting out of his car and who divorces military affairs from politics.

Revolutionary war and traditional guerrilla warfare share certain characteristics. Both depend on similar kinds of terrain, a backward society, the support of the people—and an oppressor. Both require strong and unified leadership; both require bases from which to operate. Revolutionary war begins with traditional guerrilla tactics, but thereafter it leaves guerrilla war far behind.

The first necessity for both revolutionary and guerrilla war is plenty of space traversed by few roads or railroads—preferably space filled with mountains or swamp and jungle. This is the kind of terrain that makes the man on foot who intimately knows the ground more mobile than the man in the truck with a map. It enables guerrilla groups to create base areas

out of reach of road-bound regular troops. It is fine for ambushing. Throughout history guerrillas have thrived in wild, empty country, such as North America in the eighteenth century, or even the nineteenth. The Franco-Indian ambush of General Braddock and Colonel Washington on the Monongahela in 1755 is a classic example of a guerrilla attack: the column blocked in a narrow defile, the devastating fire from both sides, the panic, the shambles. And in a general sense the whole saga of the winning of the west can be regarded as an episode in guerrilla warfare.

Europe, too, in the centuries before it became finely meshed with good roads and railroads, had the space and the natural cover for guerrillas to thrive. In the Thirty Years' War bands of armed peasants took vengeance on straying soldiery in the dark forests of Germany. The wild Balkan fringes of the Austrian empire were a great nursery of troops of highly irregular conduct and costume—for example, hussars (now domesticated into elegance) and pandours.

In the British Isles the bogs and mountains of Ireland have seen guerrillas sally forth to cut English throats for centuries. The struggle between the native Irish and Mountjoy, Elizabeth I's viceroy, in the opening years of the seventeenth century, presents a classic picture of guerrilla and antiguerrilla tactics astonishingly like that of Vietnam in our time. The English tried to cramp Irish mobility by dotting the country with fortified garrisons; they harried the Irish with fast-moving "search-and-destroy" columns. Crops were burned and cattle driven off or slaughtered in order to deprive the Irish of supplies, and villages were freely burned down to deny them shelter and support. The Highlands of Scotland sheltered tribes that practiced successful guerrilla war against the government or each other from the time of the Roman governor Agricola until they were finally smashed in the battle at Culloden in 1746.

It was Spain that gave guerrilla warfare its name (*guerrilla*—"little war") during the war against the French from 1808 to 1814; and Spain was perfect guerrilla country, abundantly furnished with unmapped mountains traversed only by goat tracks. French armies were scattered across these vast spaces, guarding the towns, trying to protect the few and vital main highways, plunging about unavailingly in the hunt for guerrillas. The guerrillas forced the French to spread their army of 230,000 men across the Iberian Peninsula, so that Wellington, with an army of only 45,000, was able to defeat what forces the French could muster to face him in a campaign.

On the whole, plains have never been considered good guerrilla country, but in South Africa the Boer commandos on their fast ponies involved the British Empire in two years of elaborate counterguerrilla campaigning from 1900 to 1902, and the deserts of Arabia were exploited during the First World War by Colonel T. E. Lawrence and his Arab guerrillas fighting against the Turkish army. Air power has probably rendered these performances in open country unrepeatable.

During the Second World War it was the nature of the local terrain that decided whether resistance against German and Italian occupation should take the form of an "underground" or of open guerrilla war. Guerrilla war was impossible in the industrialized, densely settled, heavily roaded countries of western Europe. The tangled mountains of Yugoslavia and Greece and the forests and swamps of Russia, on the other hand, provided the space and difficult terrain that major guerrilla movements thrive on.

And it was geography that in the first place permitted the debut of guerrilla war as an independent and decisive form of warfare in China in the 1930's and 1940's: geography and that other precondition, a backward country. Thus in December, 1936, Mao Tse-tung wrote: "China is a vast country—'When it is dark in the east, it is light in the west; when things are dark in the south, there is still light in the north.' Hence one need not worry about lack of room for maneuver. . . .

"China's political and economic development is uneven—a weak capitalist economy coexists with a preponderant semi-feudal economy; a few modern industrial and commercial cities coexist with a vast stagnant countryside; several million industrial workers coexist with several hundred millions of peasants and handicraftsmen . . . a few railways, steamship lines and motor roads exist side by side with a vast number of wheelbarrow paths and footpaths . . ."

In terms of guerrilla warfare space is essential, but relative; "space" is what absorbs the momentum of attack of a regular, or Western-style army. A square mile of dense tropical rain forest is space that is equivalent to many times its area of open plain. Although Vietnam and Malaya are small countries compared with China, they are still excellent ground for guerrillas because of their mountains and jungle, where a hundred feet an hour may represent fair progress. Space is the key not only to the fluid tactics of guerrillas—swift pounces followed by disappearance and dispersal—but to the very existence of the guerrilla movement. For guerrillas must have secure bases from which to operate. Space protects the guerrilla bases from counterguerrilla attack. Even if one base has to be abandoned, space enables the guerrillas to transfer to another. Bases can vary from operational camps to whole districts in remote areas that have fallen under guerrilla control and are beyond the capacity of counterguerrilla forces to reach and occupy.

Both Mao's "revolutionary war" and traditional guerrilla war need a single, effective organization with a clear chain of command; otherwise the scattered and clandestine nature of guerrilla war brings out all the personal, empire-building rivalry in human nature that can make life so Byzantine even in a regular army or a big business. In the case of Mao's revolutionary war it is the Communist Party machine that provides efficient and ruthless single direction. In the case of guerrillas operating in collaboration with a regular field army it is best that they should be under the direct orders of the army commander-in-chief in their region, because their effectiveness depends on close integration with military plans.

Both guerrilla and revolutionary war are virtually impossible without the active support or passive sympathy of all or large sections of the population. This essential point was made by Mao in a now famous simile: "Many people think it is impossible for guerrillas to exist long in the enemy's rear. Such a belief reveals a lack of comprehension of the relationship that should exist between the people and troops. The former may be likened to water and the latter to fish who inhabit it. How may it be said that these two cannot exist together?"

And elsewhere he turned the simile the other way: "With the common people of the whole country mobilized, we shall create a vast sea of humanity and drown the enemy in it."

Guerrillas depend on the population for food, shelter, emergency medical care, and even active collaboration in such activities as sabotage. The population is one of their best sources of information about enemy movements and plans: any peasant or shepherd near a road is a reconnaissance unit; any native-born person the enemy comes in contact with is a spy—telephone operators, office workers, waiters, shopkeepers, bar girls and prostitutes, transport workers. On the other hand the mute hostility of the population is a crippling handicap to the counterguerrilla army, which is starved of accurate operational intelligence about the guerrillas. The counterguerrillas move and fight in the dark—but are themselves brilliantly illuminated. This lack of a known target leads to the indiscriminate nature of so many antiguerrilla operations, and the consequent damage to the innocent only further alienates the population.

---

*"Guerrilla tactics
are founded on mobility,
fluidity, deception,
and surprise; or, in the
words of Sun Tzu,
the Chinese military writer
of ancient times,
'Uproar in the East, attack
in the West.'"*

Another characteristic shared by revolutionary war and traditional guerrilla war lies in tactics. Any kind of stand-up fight against regular troops with heavy weapons is fatal. The orthodox military principle of thumping at the enemy's center of gravity is replaced by a thoroughgoing application of what Sir Basil Liddell Hart calls the "indirect approach." Guerrilla tactics are founded on mobility, fluidity, deception, and surprise; or, in the words of Sun Tzu, the Chinese military writer of ancient times, "Uproar in the East, attack in the West." "Is the enemy strong?" writes General Giap about North Vietnam; "One avoids him. Is he weak? One attacks him." And Giap goes on to demand "initiative, suppleness, rapidity, sur-

prise, suddenness in attack and retreat . . ."

The favored objectives of such sudden attacks are well known: weakly protected convoys or detachments in narrow defiles, isolated military posts, railroad tracks and installations, airfields, military camps, power stations. Widespread but well-co-ordinated attacks can paralyze a modern army, with its dependence on vast tonnages of supply and a network of communications. Apart from specific operations such as these, however, the principal service of guerrillas in a conventional war is to distract large numbers of the enemy forces from the battle fronts.

It is here, in the ultimate strategic role and purpose of guerrilla operations, that revolutionary war according to Mao Tse-tung's theory and practice parts company with traditional guerrilla war. In traditional guerrilla war, even on as large a scale as in Yugoslavia or Russia in the Second World War, the strategic role is secondary to that of a separate conventional field army; and the purpose of the combined operations of the two kinds of force is limited to military victory in a particular war.

In revolutionary war the ultimate objective is not merely military, but political: the overthrow of an existing regime or social order. And the guerrillas themselves are the instrument of decision. It is in this conception that Mao is so original. In his writings in the 1930's he foresaw what he lived to see triumphantly carried out—an evolution of the original Chinese Communist guerrilla forces into a great field army capable of smashing the enemy (already weakened by guerrilla war) in open battle.

Mao's conception of revolutionary war stood poor old Marx on his head. In the first place it was to take place in a backward country and be rooted in the peasantry, whereas Marx prophesied that the revolution would take place in an advanced industrial country and be rooted in the urban prole-

tariat. In the second place Marx expected the workers' revolution to take the traditional revolutionary form of a sudden massive uprising, a single act of violence that would replace the old authority with the new—as in fact happened in Russia. However, in Mao's thinking, revolutionary war is a long and gradual process, a war of slow attrition that he calls "the protracted war."

Nothing could be more opposite to the Western political and military temperament than this stoic acceptance of attrition and prolonged conflict. The fallacy of the quick and easy victory—the *Blitzkrieg*—is dear to Western hearts; it was the hope with which the Union entered the Civil War, and all the belligerents went to war in 1914, and Germany went to war in 1939. It underlies the Western faith today in massed hardware—aircraft, tanks, mechanization. NATO does not dare to contemplate any kind of prolonged conflict in Europe. And yet the history of war generally proves Mao and Giap right.

Even allowing for a protracted war —ten, twenty, years—it appears at first sight to ask too much of guerillas that they should succeed in beating a regular army backed by all the resources of a government machine. Yet it has happened now more than once, and roughly in accordance with the scenario sketched by Mao in the 1930's with reference to China's struggle against the invading Japanese. Mao wrote that "it can reasonably be assumed that this protracted war will pass through three stages. The first stage covers the period of the enemy's strategic offensive and our strategic defensive. . . . At the tail end of the first stage, the enemy will be forced to fix certain terminal points to his strategic offensive owing to his shortage of troops and our firm resistance, and upon reaching them he will stop his strategic offensive and enter the stage of safeguarding his occupied areas."

During the Communists' struggle with Chiang Kai-shek and the Nationalists after the Japanese surrender in 1945, the Nationalist strategic offensive took the form of a series of grandiose attempts to overrun the Communists' base areas in central and northwestern China. The Chinese Red Army had by then already evolved from a pure guerrilla movement in the 1920's into a field army, although still without heavy weapons, and itself operated in conjunction with guerrillas. The Nationalists followed an orthodox Western-style offensive strategy, striking along railroads and highways to conquer cities and territory. It was a somewhat sleazy and ramshackle version of allied operations in Europe: air bombardment, artillery support, tanks, long supply lines, armies aligned on attacking fronts. The Communists, on the other hand, fought what Mao calls "mobile war"—guerrilla war writ large. No attempt was made to defend territory or cities, not even the Communist capital of Yenan; pitched battle with the Nationalists was evaded by timely and rapid retreat, while Communist forces attacked the Nationalist flanks and communications. If one base area was occupied, the army moved across country to another. When the Nationalists finally ran out of steam, they had failed to force any kind of decisive battle on the Communists, let alone win it.

In Indochina, at the same time, the Communist Vietminh were beginning their struggle against the French at the very beginning—small-scale guerrilla warfare from base areas in the remote mountains of northern Tonkin. Once again the first stage of the conflict saw, as Mao predicted, a massive attempt by the enemy to crush the Communists in one great offensive. The French Expeditionary Corps headed for the mountains in its trucks and tanks and half-tracks. But trying to nail the Vietminh proved to be like trying to scoop up a drop of mercury with a steel gauntlet. Whenever the French weren't looking, the Vietminh attacked and disappeared.

With the base areas and the revolu-tionary forces thus still intact, revolutionary war moves, according to Mao, into its second stage: "The second stage may be termed one of strategic stalemate . . . the enemy will attempt to safeguard the occupied areas . . . our forces will be switched in large numbers to the enemy's rear . . . and basing themselves on all the areas not actually occupied by the enemy and co-ordinating with the people's local armed forces, they will launch extensive, fierce guerrilla warfare . . ."

It is this second, or middle, stage that presents the classic pattern of revolutionary war—the shapelessness of the conflict, "no fixed line of demarcation," as Giap expresses it; "the front being wherever the enemy is found." All the President's helicopters and all the President's men are no answer to this invisibility and ubiquity of the enemy. The dilemma of the conventional soldier is well expressed by a French officer serving in Indochina:

"We hold everything, but the enemy is everywhere. If we leave the roads to fight, our vehicles bog down in the swamps and rice fields. . . . If we go on foot, we are lost in a terrible terrain of jungles, mountains and forests where malaria and dysentery are the worst of our foes. . . .

"In daylight, however, we succeed in keeping order because our planes and our vehicles can quickly bring infantry to search the jungle . . .

"By night, Indochina belongs to the Vietminh . . ."

This is the stage, in Mao's imagery, that involves drowning the enemy in a sea of people. Obviously the whole situation depends on the basic premise that the Communist revolutionaries enjoy the support of the people and the existing regime does not. And this introduces a fundamental aspect of revolutionary war and its chances of success.

A revolutionary army is not like a Western army, a purely military institution for use in regrettable contingencies, a kind of fire brigade. It is a party political instrument engaged in a political struggle. "The Chinese Red Army," wrote Mao, "is an armed body for carrying out the political tasks of the revolution." It follows that officers and men are not just professional military performers like those of a Western army; they are convinced Communists, permeated by Marxist political awareness. They undergo ceaseless indoctrination and reindoctrination. Nothing like it has been seen since Cromwell's troopers and their preachers and prayer meetings; not even in Soviet Russia or Nazi Germany.

Giap insists that "the political work in its ranks is of first importance. *It is the soul of the army.*

"The Viet Nam People's Army has been created by the party. . . . The Army has always had its political commissars."

"Thus in the direction of revolutionary war there are none of those ludicrous . . . divisions that occur in the West between soldiers and politicians, fighting and peacemaking, strategy and policy."

Nor do the leaders of revolutionary war share the Western liberal view that armed violence is a deplorable and barbarous breakdown in a desirable and natural harmony called peace. To them violence is an acceptable component in a total political strategy. Thus in the direction of revolutionary war there are none of those ludicrous and disastrous divisions that occur in the West between soldiers and politicians, fighting and peacemaking, strategy and policy.

Fighting is only one aspect of revolutionary war; the other aspect, just as important—indeed fundamentally im-

9

portant—is the political conversion of the mass of the peasantry. It is by relentless evangelizing in the villages that grievances such as land hunger, or corrupt government, or nationalist aspirations are made to work for the Communists and against the existing regime. Within the areas controlled by the Communists, efficient and honest administration, coupled with social reforms, completes the winning of the masses.

In China the Communists could exploit the hatred of the Japanese invader and the corruption and inefficiency of Chiang Kai-shek's Nationalist regime, the pillaging practiced by its undisciplined soldiery. In Vietnam they could exploit the Vietnamese desire for independence. In both China and Vietnam they could exploit the miseries of debt-ridden peasants cultivating the property of absentee landlords. And in both countries they were helped by the remoteness of the existing government machinery from the people and their needs.

The purpose of violence in this total strategy of political conversion is not only ultimately to topple the existing regime in battle. Right at the beginning of the war, it serves a direct political purpose by destroying the authority, prestige, and power to function of the local organs of the existing regime. By the murder of its district officers and by other means of intimidation and disruption, the central government is thus further split from the people.

Thus in the second, or stalemate, stage of revolutionary war the Communists hold the countryside, the people, the reality of power; the existing regime holds the cities and the main arteries of communication, the façade of power. It is the very obligation of the existing regime to defend territory, cities, and communications that hands initiative and mobility to the guerrilla forces. And it is this initiative that cancels out the huge disparity of numbers.

It is crucial to Mao's conception of the three stages of revolutionary war that operations should evolve finally from guerrilla war into major offensives. "Parallel with the gradual development from guerrilla warfare to mobile warfare," writes Giap, "and with better supply and equipment, we had, from scattered units, gradually organized concentrated ones, then regiments and divisions of a regular army."

In the third stage of protracted revolutionary war, the revolutionary forces launch "the strategic counteroffensive" against an enemy ready for the kill. "Our primary form of fighting," Mao laid down, "will still be mobile warfare, but positional warfare [i.e., Western-style battles for cities and other territorial objectives] will rise to importance."

The strategic counteroffensive falls on a weakened and demoralized army, on troops scattered in static defense of territory; it has all the elements of surprise and overwhelming local superiority derived from its guerrilla ancestry. In Manchuria in 1948, the Chinese Nationalists were locked up in the cities, cut off except for air supply, and then destroyed piecemeal. It was a disaster from which Chiang Kai-shek never recovered. In 1949 the Communist forces swept south through China in a series of great mobile battles, gaining strength as they went, from the local population and from Nationalist deserters and prisoners.

In Vietnam at the end of 1949 the Vietminh stunned the French by overwhelming the provinces along the Chinese border by "orthodox" local offensives. It was then, however, that the Vietminh made a serious blunder; they assumed that the whole French position in Indochina was now ripe for the general counteroffensive. Their attempt to overwhelm the stronghold of French power in the Red River Delta was smashed by French firepower at the battle of Vinh Yen. This setback had no effect on the Communist will for ultimate victory; they simply returned to stage two: stalemate, guerrilla war, local attacks.

The Vietminh launched their second strategic counteroffensive in Indochina in the spring of 1954, not against the Red River Delta but against the air-supplied French fortress of Dien Bien Phu. This had already come to be a showplace and a symbol of French military power, and the siege drew in many of the French Expeditionary Corps' best available field troops. The siege provides a textbook illustration of revolutionary war in its third stage. The besieging forces consisted of four field divisions and a heavy division of Russian artillery brought in through China. The appalling problem of supply over hundreds of miles of a heavily bombed mountain road was solved by mobilizing the entire population. Hundreds of thousands of peasants built and repaired roads for the Russian Molotova trucks, piloted sampans, carried supplies on their backs or on bicycles with special frames. Air power was beaten by foot power. And French firepower was locally overwhelmed by Vietminh firepower.

After the fall of Dien Bien Phu, there was no need to complete a general conquest of Vietnam; the French will had finally been broken. Following the Geneva Conference the French went quietly to their ships and home.

Wherever geographical and social conditions are favorable, revolutionary war thus poses very great dangers to those who think only in terms of military countermeasures—and the countermeasures of technological war at that. The West should not take too much comfort from its successes against revolutionary war in Greece (1946–49), the Philippines (1946–54), and Malaya (1948–60). They were especially favorable cases. In Greece and Malaya the Communists neglected the social and political aspects of their strategy; they failed to win wide enough or fanatical enough popular support. The Greeks also tried to defend their base areas by formal defensive battles instead of by mobility and evasion, and they were smashed by the firepower of the Greek army. In Greece too, Tito's rift with Stalinist Russia led to a closing of the Yugoslav frontier to the guerrillas, and the loss of a vital sanctuary and source of supply.

Malaya has very little land frontier, the Philippines none; both were in any case remote from Communist countries. In Malaya the main Communist support lay in the Chinese element of a multiracial population, principally among 500,000 squatters on the fringes of the jungle. This is very different from the sixteen million Vietnamese who wanted independence from the French. Yet victory in Malaya required twelve years and odds of twelve to one.

"Orthodox Western armed forces and heavy equipment are next to useless.... However, there is in any case no purely military solution to revolutionary warfare."

Nevertheless, there are lessons to be drawn from the experience in Malaya and the Philippines. Orthodox Western armed forces and heavy equipment are next to useless. The military answer lies in small units able to match the guerrillas in ability to live in the jungles or mountains and in the crafts of tracking and ambush. These penetration groups are supplemented by the mobility conferred by air power. They must be mobile and aggressive; they must keep the guerrillas moving, break them up.

However, there is in any case no purely military solution to revolutionary warfare; victory lies in political and social action. It lies in remedying the grievances the Communists exploit. Just as the revolutionaries try to split the people from the existing regime, so the counterguerrillas must try to

split the guerrillas from the people. Without the "water" of the mass support, the "fish" expire, denied food, supplies, and operational intelligence. In Malaya, for example, the 500,000 Chinese squatters were relocated under secure government protection in model villages, where they were "deindoctrinated" by government information teams.

The course of the second Indochina war suggests that the United States has not found an answer to revolutionary war. It seems clear that in 1965–67 the United States fell victim to the mistake that doomed the French and the Chinese Nationalists—the quest for a quick victory. Subsequently the American forces tried to make up for the lack of accurate intelligence, knowledge of the terrain, and skill in guerrilla fighting by "combine harvesting" the whole country with firepower and machine power. By sheer weight and spread this clearly did much to damage the Vietcong; you can, after all, rid your house of rats by burning it down. But the indiscriminate destruction and remote nature of technological war make nonsense of the simultaneous attempts to win the hearts of the people by social reform. The military component of American strategy was hardly well integrated into their total strategy—a fault of Western society, where politicians never think in terms of violent conflict and soldiers never think in terms of politics.

In the last resort, revolutionary war, like cholera, is best defeated before it breaks out. And it will break out again, either in Asia, South America, or Africa, where all the essential preconditions for successful guerrilla warfare now exist. The Chinese marshal Lin Piao has gone so far as to state that eventually revolutionary war will win control of the entire world: in his imagery "the city" (the industrial countries of the West) will be isolated and submerged by the "countryside" (the backward peasant regions of the rest of the world); it is the basic

strategy of revolutionary war enlarged to a global scale.

There is yet another danger—within the United States itself. There is the possibility of a mutation of the revolutionary war that will permit it to thrive in the great industrial conurbations. Marx believed that the proletarian revolution would occur in an advanced urban capitalist society having extremes of wealth and poverty; America fits this description probably better than any other Western country. But the Negro minority is not only an urban proletariat; it is (or thinks it is) an oppressed "colonial" people, like the Algerians or the Vietnamese. Both of the great dynamic forces of revolutionary war—economic exploitation and nationalism—are therefore present inside American society. Marx believed the revolution would take the form of a single act of violence in the industrial cities; Mao changed this to a continuing war of attrition in the countryside. It might be possible to mix Mao and Marx and have a continuing war of attrition in the cities. The cities could provide "asphalt jungles" for ambush and concealment; the Negro ghettos the secure base areas.

So far the Negro masses of America have not displayed the necessary self-discipline and organization for revolutionary war, nor have leaders of the quality of Mao or Giap or even Castro emerged. However, if Negro grievances are not swiftly and completely remedied, the shapeless and spontaneous outbreaks of violence, arson, and looting may change into a planned and controlled strategy aimed at destroying existing authority in the Negro areas of American cities. Against such a strategy, force alone could prove no better an answer in America than it has proved elsewhere in the world.

Correlli Barnett is an English military historian. He wrote the article "On the Raising of Armies" appearing in the Summer, 1968, issue of HORIZON.

THE HOUR
OF THE OX

"…now, many of the homes of the
people were destroyed by the
spreading flames, and there were
none but did lament, saying,
'What has become of the world?'"

—from *The Tale of Heiji*

The scroll painting of the burning of the Sanjo Palace, above, depicts in narrative form the attack of rebel warriors in 1160 on the residence of the retired Japanese emperor Go-Shirakawa. Viewed from right to left, the seven-hundred-year-old scroll shows, first, the attackers and onlookers rushing headlong to the palace, while in the demarcated center portion—reproduced on the following pages in a color foldout—the ex-

"At about the hour of the ox" (around 2 A.M.) on the night of the ninth day of the twelfth month of the year 1159—or January 19, 1160, according to the Western calendar— a body of more than five hundred mounted, armor-clad men stormed the Sanjo Palace (literally the "Third Avenue Palace") in the capital city of Kyoto in Japan and made away with the retired emperor Go-Shirakawa. It was a colorful incident, especially as seen through the artist's eye; but it had a sordid background of rivalries for power between members of the imperial family, between members of the great family of Fujiwara nobles who dominated the royal court, and between various groups of military men the Fujiwara used to back up their conflicting claims—the "claws and teeth" of the Fujiwara, as the chroniclers called them.

The winning side in the Sanjo Palace affair proved to be the losers in the little war the incident provoked, known by the name of the "year period" as the Heiji War. And in turn, the winners in the Heiji War proved to be the ultimate losers in the series of wars between 1156 and 1185 that brought all of Japan for the first time under the control of feudal warriors.

One might conclude that the attack on the Sanjo Palace, for all its color and drama, was a meaningless episode— part of a crazy-quilt pattern of feudal violence. But seen in broader perspective, it was a turning point in history, symbolic of the great, wrenching change Japan underwent in the twelfth century, and it put the country on a different course from the rest of Asia.

For three and a half centuries before the wars that started in 1156, the emperors had reigned in peace from their palaces in Kyoto. Most of this time, though, the actual power had been in the hands of the Fujiwara family, whose members had appropriated for themselves the top offices in the government. One means by which they maintained control over the emperors was by marrying their daughters to the emperors and persuading the latter to retire from the burdensome ceremonial tasks of their position in favor of their infant sons of Fujiwara mothers. This left the young emperors under the dominance of the Fujiwara grandfathers, who controlled affairs of state as regents for underage emperors and as chancellors for adult ones. The Fujiwara, however, never tried to usurp the throne and continued to recognize that their own authority derived from the emperors.

This left the door open for ambitious emperors to strike back, and in the latter half of the eleventh century successive retired emperors had managed to win back control of the court, though the Fujiwara continued to occupy the posts of regent and chancellor.

Actually neither the emperors nor the Fujiwara exerted much control over most of Japan. The Japanese had borrowed, along with a good deal of China's higher culture, its centralized and bureaucratic form of government as well; but by the twelfth century most of the land had drifted off the tax registers and into tax-free estates under the control of local managers. These men paid the revenues due the ultimate owners of the estates, usually courtier families or religious establishments near the capital, but they banded together in individual fighting groups—vigilantes, we might have called them—to maintain law and order locally.

Such military cliques usually centered around men having special hereditary prestige. Often these were descendants of cadet branches of the imperial family who, under the new family names of Minamoto or Taira, had gone to the provinces to seek their fortunes as local officials. One Mina-

By EDWIN O. REISCHAUER

emperor is being enticed into a waiting carriage. The warriors then burst into the palace, set fire to its buildings, and slaughter the robed courtiers. Opposite, at far left, they ride off with the kidnapped emperor, led by an officer on a rearing steed; the horse and rider are shown in a detail on pages 12–13. Done in water colors on paper, the scroll, which is nearly twenty-three feet long, may be the greatest of all Japanese battle pictures.

moto line had risen to great prominence in a series of wars in northern Japan in the eleventh century and by the twelfth was firmly entrenched in eastern Japan, while a Taira family had similarly established its predominance in western Japan.

The warrior bands under the leadership of the Minamoto or Taira consisted of the provincial aristocracy, and their profession as fighting men was an aristocratic one; in Japan, as in medieval Europe, the basic fighting unit was a mounted, armored knight, and it took considerable wealth to maintain the necessary equipment. The weapons and armor of a Japanese knight, however, were quite different from those of his European counterpart. He was expert at shooting arrows from horseback, and for close combat he relied solely on a long, curved sword, made of what was at this time already the finest steel produced in the world. His armor looked flimsy and even frivolous in its gay colors, compared to that worn in the West, but it was probably more efficient. Made for the most part of thin, overlapping strips of steel held together by colored thongs and draped loosely over the body, it was much lighter than a European suit of armor and allowed far greater freedom of movement.

Although the rival bands of provincial warriors established their military supremacy in various parts of Japan, they made no effort to control the imperial court or central government. At Kyoto courtiers maintained the sophisticated and highly aesthetic way of life so beautifully described by an early eleventh-century court lady in *The Tale of Genji*, the world's first real novel and still one of its greatest. It portrays an aristocratic society existing not just in peace and luxury but completely absorbed in literary and artistic expression and gracious living. Poetry was a passion with these people. So also were court and religious ritual and the art of love-making.

This gentle, urbane way of life came to an abrupt end in the middle of the twelfth century, when rival contenders for dominance within the imperial family and the Fujiwara called in the provincial warriors to help them settle their disputes. The resulting wars revealed that the real power had in fact shifted from the emperors and their courtiers to the provincial military. Viewed in this historical perspective, the incident at the Sanjo Palace takes on new meaning. The abduction of the retired emperor by the armored knights is symbolic of the seizure of power by the provincial military. As

they ride away with their captive, the whole country rides with them into a great new chapter of Japanese history.

The wars between 1156 and 1185 that marked the transition to feudalism immediately became a favorite theme for storytellers and chanters of ballads. These tales and ballads were written down in a variety of textual forms. Those concerning the Heiji War of the winter of 1159–1160 were appropriately called *The Tale of Heiji* (*Heiji monogatari*) and probably date from the early decades of the thirteenth century.

Scroll paintings based on the major incidents recounted in *The Tale of Heiji* were also made a generation or two later, perhaps between 1249 and 1287, and of these, three remain. The scroll depicting the attack on the Sanjo Palace is owned by the Museum of Fine Arts in Boston and is not only the finest of the three Heiji scrolls but in many ways the best example of Japanese scroll painting to be found outside of Japan. The flow of the story it portrays; its marvelous sense of composition, from the opening rush of onlookers toward the palace to the final scene of the withdrawing warriors, the lead figure walking with half-drawn bow pointing to the future; the many vivid individual actions; the explosive force of the fire as it consumes the highly inflammable wooden palace buildings—all make this one of the most exciting and convincing artistic portrayals of a battle scene of any time or place.

Painted a hundred years or more after the attack, the scroll cannot be accepted as a reliable picture of the actual incident. But Japanese costumes and accoutrements had changed little in the intervening century. Our artist thus has given us in a general sense an accurate and brilliantly detailed portrayal of the seizure of power by the rising feudal military class and the attendant destruction of the old court society and its palaces.

The historical incidents leading to the attack on the Sanjo Palace are complicated. When the retired emperor who had been exercising ultimate power in Kyoto died in 1156, a struggle for leadership ensued within both the imperial family and the Fujiwara. In a brief war that summer the victors were the reigning emperor Go-Shirakawa, over his elder brother, a retired emperor, and the Fujiwara chancellor, over a younger brother who had challenged his leadership of the family. More significantly, one of the warrior cliques called in to fight the war—the Taira, led by Kiyomori together with Yoshitomo, one of the Minamoto leaders—had defeated and executed the leaders of the other cliques, who were Yoshitomo's father and brothers.

Yoshitomo, however, feeling overshadowed by his Taira allies, soon became dissatisfied with his share in the spoils, and new troubles developed within the imperial and Fujiwara families. Go-Shirakawa abdicated in 1158 in favor of his son Nijo, but retained control of the court for himself. Friction soon developed between the retired emperor and the ruling emperor, encouraged by ambitious though relatively minor Fujiwara nobles, Nobuyori supporting Nijo and Shinzei supporting the retired emperor. Yoshi-

tomo was recruited to the former's cause, and five days after Kiyomori and the other Taira partisans left Kyoto on a pilgrimage to a famous Shinto shrine, Yoshitomo led his men in the late-night attack on the Sanjo Palace, which was Go-Shirakawa's residence.

The picture scroll opens with a mad dash of nobles in their oxcarts and common citizens and soldiers on foot to the scene of the fighting. *The Tale of Heiji* says nothing about a throng of onlookers at the battle, and it seems improbable that there was one for a sneak attack in the middle of the night, but it makes a moving opening scene, nonetheless. We next find the attacking force inside the palace with a carriage drawn up to a palace building for the retired emperor to enter. Then comes the scene of the destruction of the palace and its inmates, which *The Tale of Heiji* relates as follows:

The situation at the Sanjo Palace was beyond description. Soldiers were guarding all the gates, and flames were shooting up here and there. Wild flames filled the heavens, and a tempestuous wind swept up clouds of smoke. The nobles, courtiers, and even the ladies-in-waiting of the women's quarters were shot down or slashed to death . . . When they rushed out, so as not to be burned by the fire, they met with arrows. When they turned back, so that they would not be struck by the arrows, they were consumed by the flames. Those who were afraid of the arrows and terrified by the flames even jumped into the wells in large numbers, and of these, too, the bottom ones in a short time had drowned, those in the middle had been crushed to death by their fellows, and those on top had been burned up by the flames themselves. The palace buildings, built one beside the other, were swept by a fierce wind, and ashes spewed forth upon the ground. . . .

The last part of the scroll shows the attackers withdrawing with their captive. Two heads are carried on pikes by foot soldiers. These are presumably the heads of Oe Ienaka and Taira Yasutada (in East Asia family names always precede given names), who are men-

TEXT CONTINUED ON PAGE 25

A SCENE OF HORROR TRANSFORMED INTO ART

In the foldout opposite the scroll's superb combination of sweeping mass movement and meticulous rendering of individual combatants is clearly seen. The action proceeds from right to left (or back to front), and the first two pages show the luring of the retired emperor into a carriage drawn up to his veranda. The pale blue figure of the treacherous courtier Nobuyori is dimly seen at the door of the imperial apartment, while his warrior ally Yoshitomo, near the carriage, gives commands to his impatient minions. The center pages depict the scene of carnage within the rapidly burning palace, where the hopelessly trapped courtiers are shot, trampled, and hacked to death without mercy. A well is clogged with the bodies of those who had leaped into it in terror. Other horsemen rush toward the gate to join their comrades outside. The last pages (opposite) show the attackers, some carrying severed heads as trophies, remassing beyond the gates, their cruel mission having been swiftly completed. The scroll's detail is unsparing, certainly, yet the horrors depicted remain strictly subordinate to the artist's perennial concern with line, mass, and color. As a result, the unknown creator of The Burning of the Sanjo Palace *has transmuted his subject into a work of decorative beauty.*

16

FOLDOUT (TO BE VIEWED FROM BACK TO FRONT) →

TEXT CONTINUED FROM PAGE 16

tioned as having lost their lives in defense of the palace. Beside seven of the horsemen are empty cartouches, no doubt designed to contain the names of the leading attackers, including Yoshitomo and Nobuyori, but no one ever filled them in.

On hearing the news of the abduction of the retired emperor, Kiyomori and his Taira henchmen returned in haste to the capital, and the stage was now set for the climactic battles of the Heiji War. The Taira stormed the main imperial palace, where the Minamoto forces had ensconced themselves. In the battle the Fujiwara noble Nobuyori showed himself to be a craven coward, unable even to sit his horse properly. Or at least so the thirteenth-century author describes him; but we must remember that, writing when he did, he was strongly prejudiced in favor of the newly dominant warrior class. He dwells in loving detail on the colorful suits of armor and high-spirited mounts of the warrior leaders and recounts with obvious pride their personal exploits. Thus the author describes the entrance into battle of Yoshihira, one of the Minamoto leaders, as follows:

Raising his voice, he shouted, "Announce that we may hear who is the general on your side. He who speaks is one called Kamakura no Akugenda Yoshihira, descendant in the ninth generation of the Emperor Seiwa and eldest son of . . . Yoshitomo. In my many wars since the age of fifteen when I . . . smote my uncle Yoshikata . . . never have I been called inadequate. Come face me, now aged nineteen." And he smashed his way into the very midst of the five hundred horsemen.

The Minamoto managed with difficulty to repulse the Taira onslaught, but as they pursued the withdrawing attackers, other Taira forces seized the now deserted imperial palace. The fighting spread throughout the city but proved inconclusive. When the Minamoto a few days later attacked the Taira headquarters in the south-

eastern corner of the city, they were defeated and started a long retreat northward from the city, during which they were eventually crushed and Yoshitomo and his two eldest sons were killed.

Kiyomori and his followers now found themselves in complete control of the court and without serious military rivals in the country. They settled down at the capital, taking high government posts for themselves. Kiyomori even followed the old Fujiwara practice of marrying his daughter to the emperor and had the satisfaction of placing his own grandson on the throne in 1180. But in turning themselves into courtiers the Taira leaders lost touch with their provincial supporters, and when remnants of the Minamoto faction rallied in eastern Japan, the Taira found themselves gravely threatened.

Yoshitomo's third son, Yoritomo, who was only thirteen at the time of the Heiji War, had been spared and had been put under the care of a Taira partisan in east Japan. Yoritomo became the center of the general uprising of former Minamoto partisans in 1180. In the five-year war that followed, the Minamoto established a firm grip on all of east Japan, seized the capital, and drove the Taira down the Inland Sea in a series of relentless battles, finally destroying them along with Kiyomori's imperial grandson in a great sea battle at Dan no Ura at the western end of the Inland Sea.

Yoritomo thus succeeded to control of the imperial court and of all Japan, but he avoided the Taira error of settling down in the effete capital and adopting the ways of the old court aristocracy. Instead, under the title of shogun, he claimed only to head the military arm of the old imperial government, and he established his own "tent government," a term meaning a government not of civilian courtiers but of military men, at Kamakura, which was in his own regional base of power in east Japan. The shift in the

control of Japan from emperors and court aristocrats to feudal warriors was now complete. The ride of the knights with their imperial captive from the Sanjo Palace was now at an end, and Japan had crossed the watershed into feudalism.

For a century and a half (1185–1333) Japan was ruled efficiently from Kamakura in what might be called a protofeudal system. With the further growth of the feudal class, however, the Kamakura system fell apart, and for the next two centuries Japan experienced the sort of feudal anarchy that characterized medieval Europe. Not until the late sixteenth century was the country effectively unified again, this time in a highly organized and increasingly "bureaucratic" political system within a basically feudal framework. The "tent government" of the Tokugawa family (1603–1867), established in Edo, the modern Tokyo, was far more advanced and efficient than anything known to feudal Europe, and it lasted until Japan's next great transformation—into a modern state—in the second half of the nineteenth century.

The wars of the twelfth century therefore marked the beginning of seven centuries of feudal rule. During this long period the Japanese developed the habits of hard work, the deep sense of duty, the drive for achievement, the genius for organization, the skill in complex personal relations, and the other characteristics that help to explain their huge success in recent times. The attackers of the Sanjo Palace may have brought Japan not only into feudalism but, through this apparent detour in history, significantly along the road to where it stands today as the most modernized nation outside of the Occident and the third largest industrial power in the world.

Our former ambassador to Japan, Edwin O. Reischauer is now University Professor and a member of the East Asian Research Center at Harvard.

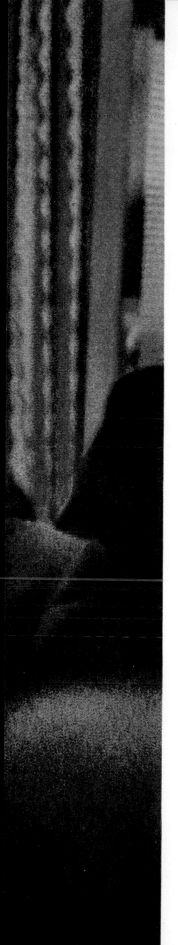

Wales?

Dominated by England for seven centuries,
yet she remains a separate nation;
bombarded by homogenizing mass media, yet she
retains her own arcane language;
a day's drive from swinging London, yet she
will always be a world away

In an age unsympathetic to quirks, when even eccentricity must be modish, the anomalous nation is more than ever a rarity. Most peoples and countries nowadays fall dutifully into a political or ethnological slot, and idiosyncratic languages, customs, and loyalties are fading almost everywhere. The Basques and Catalans are fairly subdued. The innumerable lesser races of Russia—Tartars, Mongols, Uzbeks, Ukrainians—seem to be settled into a docile mold and are demonstrated to tourists with ideological smirks. The nationalist aspirations of minorities like the Bretons or the Cornish are more quaint than formidable and seem chiefly to excite scholars of unapproachable erudition or agreeably picturesque cranks.

On the western flank of England (itself a nation not easily reduced to category) there thrives one little country whose presence, spirit, and even *raison d'être* are all unquenchably anomalous. It has defied nearly seven centuries of foreign domination to preserve its paradoxical identity, and it has acquired in the process a pungency of style that is altogether its own. Fewer than three million Welshmen live in Wales, but hundreds of thousands of people who feel themselves to be Welsh are scattered throughout the world; and everywhere, in their manner of speaking or singing or drinking, in their often evasive tactics of life and their tangential approach to human contact, they reflect the dappled presence of their homeland. Wales has survived as a nation not by beating a drum or flagwaving but by a poetic instinct, a subtle gift of adaptation, and a neverfailing flair for showmanship.

Ever since travelers began to write about Wales, they have been struck by the elusive quality of the place. It is a very beautiful country, but strange. Most of it is hilly, but the bare Welsh moorlands have none of the easygoing lushness of the English countryside to the east, whose moist green wholesomeness made Samuel Butler feel he was living in the heart of a lettuce. There is soft enough

PHOTOGRAPHS IAN BERRY—MAGNUM

Above, a crumbling barn bears the smeared slogan of the militant Welsh nationalists, now raising the cry for an independent Wales. Left, a cloth-capped Welshman still cleaving to the old musical ways sings lustily for his cronies at his local pub in Aberdare.

By JAMES MORRIS

country on the edge of Wales, in the delectably wooded Wye Valley or up on the Shropshire marches; but the upland area of the country is sparse and almost savage, giving an impression of space and sometimes of desolation quite out of proportion to its size. The culmination of Wales, in terrain as in symbolism, is the grand cluster of mountains around Snowdon in the north—which never reach 4,000 feet but nevertheless seem to have the stature of great peaks, so nobly and mistily do they stand above the sea.

Even the industrial regions of Wales have a particular flavor. The Welsh have little sense of urban elegance, and their villages are among the drabbest in Europe; yet the slate-quarry towns of the northern counties or the coal valleys of the south, blackened by generations of grime and poverty, sunk like brick-walled chasms in the hills—even these stark memorials of industrial progress possess a distinctive wry strength, inhabited as they are by huge close-knit families bound together irrevocably by hardship, cups of tea, willow-pattern china, and family jokes. In Old English the word "Welsh" meant "foreigner," but the Welsh call themselves "Cymry," meaning "comrades," and much of the atmosphere of Wales springs from a sense of inner collusion—members only, or passes must be shown.

The country is poor. Its regions are awkwardly separated by severe mountain country or by fjordlike inlets from the sea, so that driving from north to south is always laborious, and working out a railway itinerary is an intellectual challenge. The industry of Wales, like its population, is concentrated in the south, around the coal mines. Many of the harsher rural areas

AEROFILMS, LONDON

The Welsh stronghold Castell y Bere in north Wales was built about 1230, during the nation's last stand against the English. In 1295, thirteen years after Wales fell, Welsh guerrillas apparently destroyed it.

are sadly depopulated, their hill farms run-down or deserted, their country life reduced to a threadbare combination of television and traditionalism. The bigger towns are so scattered that the University of Wales maintains campuses in four places. Cardiff, the capital, is on the southern coast; the National Library is at Aberystwyth, halfway up the country.

Yet Wales is a nation. Since the sixteenth century it has been formally united with England, and its electors send their representatives to Parliament in Westminster. The laws of England apply to Wales too: the Welsh Office is in London. But Wales remains far more than a mere administrative region. It is an ethnic entity, peopled chiefly by descendants of the original Britons, popularly lumped together as Celts, who were forced into these remote western fastnesses by the Saxon invaders of prehistory. Though many English people have gone to live in Wales down the generations, and though a good deal of non-

sense is spoken about Celtic traits and sensibilities, still this is unmistakably a separate people; a more sensual people than the down-to-earth English, an airier people, less marked by inheritances of class and wealth, more obviously responsive to history.

Everybody knows the Welshman of tradition and caricature, at once comic, gifted, and suspect. He has been made fun of or stereotyped for centuries, from Shakespeare's valiant Fluellen—"All the water in Wye cannot wash your Majesty's Welsh plood out of your pody, I can tell you that"—to the pasteboard heroines of the depression tearjerkers bravely concealing the worst from their husbands, as they take the last rasher of bacon from the cupboard. Nearly everyone knows, too, the Welshman in exile, for he is all too likely to burst into old Welsh songs just before the bars close and is often an irrepressible declaimer of Welsh reminiscence.

The Welshman is a man of a particular kind, branded whether he likes it or not by a unique culture. He may be a patrician sheep farmer from the northern hills, a patriarch of the Castilian sort, grave of speech, dry of humor, dignified by harsh weather, hard country, and a puritanical faith. He may be a steelworker from the south, chiefly interested in football, beer, and the family car, with a richly fluent tongue and an eye for the girls. In either incarnation he is unmistakably a Welshman: as different from his English neighbor as a collie from a cocker spaniel, or, more pertinently, an onion from a rose.

The unmarked frontier of this nation is within a hundred and fifty miles of London, and over that frontier, oddest of all, it still speaks its own language. Despite all the pressures of conformity in the overcrowded British Isles, enmeshed in cars, swamped with newspapers, soaked in television, a quarter of the population of Wales still speaks Welsh. In some parts of Wales this original language of the Britons remains overwhelmingly the medium of everyday speech. Speaking it is no *sine qua non* of Welshness, however: there are eminent Welsh families who abandoned it generations ago, and many distinguished Welshmen of our own time—Dylan Thomas, for example—have not spoken it. There is almost nobody left in Wales who does not understand English too.

The rhythms and inflections of Welsh, though, color every Welshman's speech and thought. Its exotic sounds dramatize the Welshness of Wales and make the Englishman feel, as he travels from the intimacy of his own shires toward the wild mountains of the west, that he is truly entering a foreign country. The reassuring old place-names grow fewer as he approaches the invisible frontier. Gloucester or Ludlow give way, in the long-disputed country of the marches, to Llangattock-nigh-Usk, or World's End, or Pont-y-Bodkin; and then, as the mountains close in; as the faces of the people grow a little darker, or more intense, or more withdrawn; as the slate-gray villages stare back coldly at his passing car and the smell of woodsmoke seeps through his window; as the spindle-shanked sheep scuttle away into the dusk, with their long, dangling tails and their springy step, or the lights go on in the high mountain-farms, isolated like strongholds far above the road—then in his headlights he sees only the cabalistic place-names of the Welsh: Pentre-

Aneurin Bevan

Dylan Thomas

Richard Burton

David Lloyd George

Famed Welshmen include Britain's fiery Labor leader Nye Bevan; her great World War I prime minister, Lloyd George; poet Dylan Thomas; and actor Richard Burton, son of a coal miner named Jenkins.

dwfr, Llechrydau, Llansantffraid ym-Mechain, Rhyd y-croesau, weird unpronounceable alien names that seem to speak of arcane destinations and are devilishly hard for a chap to follow.

Myth swirls through Wales and keeps the susceptible stranger permanently bemused. This is Arthurian country. Merlin was a Welshman and according to some legends, Carmarthen-born—the first of a long line of Welsh wizards. Merlin was consulted when King Vortigern wished to sprinkle with the blood of a fatherless child the foundations of his castle on Snowdon. Merlin went to sea with nine Welsh bards in a boat made of glass. Merlin lay with the thirteen treasures of Britain in a crystal house on the Welsh isle of Bardsey. As for Arthur, everybody of open mind knows that he fought his battles and laid the trails of his chivalry in Wales.* To the Welsh he was the first of the national champions, resisting the Saxon invaders from England; and Camelot lay somewhere among the

* For the non-Welsh, archaeologists' point of view on Arthur see "The Search for King Arthur," Summer, 1968.

mountains of the north, to be glimpsed by poets and visionary shepherds on long Welsh summer evenings.

A legendary army of Welsh princes follows Arthur's footsteps, sometimes given substance by historical record. These were Welshmen of the heroic age—the Age of Princes. In ancient times Wales was a mesh of independent kingdoms, often fighting each other over deathless issues of heredity, estate, or honor and only forced into alliance by threats from outside. The Romans came and went again; the Saxons gave way to the Normans; the fissiparous Welsh society, high-flown and epic, did not greatly change its character from one age to the next. The majority of Welshmen were independent freemen, each equal to the next; but they owed complex clan loyalties to their local sovereigns, and the life of each community centered upon its princely court.

If we are to believe the traditions, these royal Welshmen of old lived lives of cultivated enlightenment, honoring the Christian creed, taking pleasure in music and poetry, feasting on fine Welsh meats and wines from the Continent. If the picture has grown rosier with the years, certainly the lyrics that have come down to us from the Middle Ages seem to show that this remote and isolated people had mastered, for all the austerity of the environment, many secrets of the civilized condition.

Although the princes have vanished, along with most of their castles, and even the names of their little dominions survive only by courtesy, so to speak, as administrative divisions, still the poems of the Welsh Golden Age remain to us. Their seductive rhythms and piquant devices prove how sensi-

TEXT CONTINUED ON PAGE 116

PHOTOGRAPHS BRUCE DAVIDSON—MAGNUM

A Portfolio of Welsh Photographs

By Bruce Davidson

At the gate of his scraggly homestead, right, a Welsh shepherd stands with his sheep dog, his bicycle, and two bold turkeys. The setting is rugged Caernarvonshire, in rural northern Wales not far from Mount Snowdon. To the Welsh themselves, this is "Welsh Wales," where Welsh is the first language, English a reluctant second, and people from the next village are described as coming "from Off." The contrast between this rural, chapel-going Wales and the mining and steel towns of the south, where the majority of Welshmen reside, is considered a striking one—to a Welshman. Yet, to a sensitive observer such as photographer Bruce Davidson, the two Wales' look very much like one nation, not so easily divisible. The homely dishevelment of a rural homestead bears a clear family resemblance to the homely dishevelment of a steel town in the south; the instinctive theatricality of the shepherd holding aloft his dog is surely echoed in the proud postures struck by the southern Welsh coal miners seen on pages 34–35. Both pictures are among the portraits taken by Mr. Davidson in a search for that durable Welsh spirit that has survived conquest, repression, industrialization, and now even television.

On a grassy knoll above Ebbw Vale, once the impoverished constituency of the spellbinding Nye Bevan, a wed-

ding party turns its back for a moment on the mills, the coke ovens, and the fumes of a Welsh industrial town

Above, a frail-looking Welsh housewife stops warily on one of the steep, grim streets that line the narrow valleys of the south of Wales. Right, after a day spent in a sunless colliery a group of miners from Rhymney rest, in monumental pride, on a heap of rubble. An aristocracy of hard labor, the coal miners of Wales used to look upon jobs in the country's new steel mills and foundries as "woman's work." Today, however, fewer and fewer men are employed to dig out the soft coal that once was used to fuel the British navy.

A boy from the manufacturing town of Merthyr Tydfil in Glamorganshire strays into the weeds of an unkempt cemetery

while his friends look on. Behind them stand a characteristic feature of industrial Wales: long brick rows of workmen's houses

Above, in a kitchen washroom decorated with a floral design, miners of Rhymney take turns washing off the day's coal dust at an antiquated tub. Right, a young Welsh schoolboy in striped tie and blazer seems out of place on the road that overlooks the smoky valley of the Ebbw River—where men of his parents' generation were content to toil heavily for long hours, grow cabbages in their back yards, and find gaiety in the fellowship of the local pub.

THINGS

ARE IN THE SADDLE

We cannot take them with us, but it seems they can take us with them

A French sociologist named Georges Perec has written a novel called *Les Choses* that has recently been published in this country under the title *Les Choses*, which goes to show how international things are becoming. The novel, essentially an elaborately embroidered household inventory, sold 100,000 copies in France and won one of their innumerable literary prizes, the Prix Renaudot. It is about a young couple called Jérôme and Sylvie, who must be one of the most boring couples in French, or any other, literature. These young people are impressed by things, all sorts and manner of things, so long as they bespeak the good life, which to them is the life of the upper classes (though they also seem to settle for what we might call Upper Bohemian); and they are voyeurs, because they are too lazy to earn enough money to buy the things they letch after. I am devoted to things myself, up to a point, but I left Jérôme and Sylvie staring into a shop window along about page fifty, and I hope never to meet them again.

One thing that 100,000 Frenchmen are not wrong about is that this is an age uncommonly concerned with things, with their manufacture, their distribution, their acquisition. Things are endowed with mystical powers beyond the dreams of those who make them, with social influence, political significance, international prestige. The world has become, if you will excuse the expression, a *thingdom*; and the importance of its several provinces is more and more determined by how many things they can make, consume, waste, and have left over to sell (or, even better, to give) to other provinces. In general, things (more viable today than ideas) are divided into two principal categories—consumer goods and military hardware—and it is a tossup which has more international status. The great debate in most provinces of thingdom is which category shall be allocated the greater part of the wealth.

It is infra dig for a "great nation" today not to have the most destructive thing of all, and scientific progress (or "who's ahead") is measured by how many things a nation can put in orbit and how big they are. Less great nations settle for dams to create power to make things, and emerging nations momentarily settle for a jet transport (which is called an airline) or a railroad: things that will transport other things when there are any to transport. Total progress is measured by improved "standard of living," which, of course, is measured primarily by things —refrigerators, clothes, automobiles, houses, furniture—not by education, say, or health. We even take nonthings like food and by processing them, freezing them, packaging them, make them into things. A thing is easier to cope with than a fact of nature in the raw. You can store it, break it, put it on the mantelpiece, forget it. If you can't think of anything else to do with it you can use it, or if you're a great nation you can negotiate about not using it.

There is a story of a little boy who was given a couple of chocolate rabbits at Easter that, I think, must have a profound meaning for our thing-ridden society. By the end of the day the rabbits had disappeared, and the boy's mother asked him what had become of them. "They got too dirty to play with," he said, "so I ate them."

If more of us could establish as logical and direct a relationship with things as this, think what a different world we would live in. There are some people who give the appearance of staying a pace or two ahead of things, men for example whose desks are always neat and uncluttered, tidy altars ornamented with the ritual accoutrements of business—the onyx-based pen stand with gold swivels, the monogrammed silver frame with pictures of wife and children, the tooled leather portfolio, the empty "in" and the full "out" baskets, symbols of decisiveness, of mastery over things. I am suspicious of such desks and darkly believe that beneath their pristine surfaces the

drawers groan with indecisions—undigested memorandums, knots of rubber bands, dried-up erasers, pennies, unused date books with one's name stamped on them in gold letters by insurance brokers: things, in other words, that are in *my* desk and seem impossible to throw away and, no matter how dirty, are impossible to eat.

We are creatures of clutter in an age of clutter. Clutter is what happens to things when they become useless but friendly. The Victorians made it into an ideal of decoration, a nice try at turning man's natural instinct for indecision into a domestic virtue of sorts. Emerson, who lived through the height of that Age of Clutter said, "Things are in the saddle, and ride mankind." The history of civilization is the history of things—things made of stone, of bronze, of iron, of clay and glass and precious metals, things for survival and for vanity. The history of mankind is one big desk drawer.

I sometimes think that the world would be a better (certainly a more orderly) place if man could "take it with him" to the grave—especially his indecisions. Consider, for example, the problem of the wire clothes hangers. Do you save them or throw them away? Or do you save the ones with the cardboard still on them and throw the others away? It is a little thing, but it is symptomatic. There is something of the pack rat in all of us.

We are forced, however, to make decisions about things lest we be defeated by them, lest, as consumers, we become consumed, buried, overwhelmed. Every so often one has to turn over a new leaf, start fresh, face the facts, and perform (or try to) other such clichés of salvation. This very day I am going to start ruthlessly throwing away things, and as a symbol of my emancipation, the first thing I am going to throw away is *Les Choses*.

Russell Lynes is a Contributing Editor to Harper's *magazine and the author of, among other things,* The Tastemakers.

By RUSSELL LYNES

DRAWINGS FOR HORIZON BY CHAS B SLACKMAN

THE GRAND ACQUISITOR

If Things make up the shape of Time, there squats the pack rat, mocking us from the hourglass

Here is a nervous, black-eyed pack rat: nut gatherer, thief, and collector in the most active sense of the word. If he can carry it or drag it, he collects it, he stores it, he hoards it. He is supremely a creature of things, of utterly useless things, of things that trip him as he scuttles for his daily bread.

His brown fur sleek, his stomach white, his long tail bushy, he looks more like a chipmunk or a squirrel than a rat, and it seems a pity that science calls him a wood rat.

He belongs to a phenomenally successful order of mammals, *Rodentia*, two thousand species of which, like one other mammal, teem everywhere on earth except at the poles and on distant desert islands. Rodents all do their separate things; while the pack rat is collecting, others are burrowing with similar zeal, or jumping or swimming with equal energy, and a few have even learned to fly. The pack rat is a member of the *Cricetidae* family, the genus *Neotoma*, and has, in twenty-two species, fitted himself into a variety of habitats from Guatemala to British Columbia, from the deserts of Arizona to the Alleghenies.

As successful as he is, he appears a bit schizophrenic to the human observer. He is ostensibly a vegetarian; however, he has no trouble switching to meals of lizards or warblers or young rabbits when the opportunity arises. He is beaverlike in his propensity for girdling small trees, lopping down shrub branches to drag off to his nest. But in times of danger he becomes a rabbit and hammers his feet on the ground in warning. With a coyote, a fox, or dog, or owl, or mammalogist at his nest he may skin up a tree faster than a squirrel. He has the eye of a crow for shiny things, including alarm clocks, dishpans, watches, money; but unlike the crow his fascina-

By FRANKLIN RUSSELL

tion for manufactured objects is not discriminating, and he collects shotgun shells with the same zeal as hair curlers. He has even been known to drag away the traps that are set to catch *him*.

He is, in short, endearing in his affinity for man's works, but infuriating in his ingenuity in converting them to his purposes. He has a mythology, attributed to him by trappers, miners, and campers. He has, they say, a sense of morality in that when he steals one item, he leaves another in its place. These people call him a trade rat, but they do not quite understand that his commerce is unwitting, made so by an agony of choice that makes him drop one stolen item when he sees another, more larcenable piece. He is the totally indiscriminating thief, a tiny Willie Sutton who cannot spend the loot he has stolen.

One pack rat, working a girls' dormitory lodge in the Cascade mountains of Washington, gives us a profile of the schizophrenic pack-thief. He stole an onion peel, a piece of bacon rind, some figs, lemons, beans, potatoes, and peanuts; and we may understand all this, even the lemons, as evidence of a catholic appetite. But what did he want with handkerchiefs, stockings, and string, when his nest was already made up nicely with a shredded comforter? We might go along with his acquisition of cantaloupe rind, bread crusts, puffballs, and biscuits, but remain baffled at his interest in a newspaper clipping on forest fires.

He went on a ten-bar chocolate binge, and we can identify with this. He went into the dried apricot business, but surely he must have gagged on half a dozen bars of soap after the apricots. He went after candles with a really ratlike hunger for tallow; but no self-respecting rat would have followed this with a sugar chaser—fifteen lumps packed into his capacious cheek pouches. This dormitory *Neotoma* wound up his thieving with a shining coffee-can cover, perhaps to examine the reflection of such a smart fellow.

To be missing a sense of enough is the lot of the pack rat (and one other important mammal), and his nest—up to twenty feet off the ground, a tangle of twigs, thorns, and grass—may bulge with hundreds of trivial items scattered through its maze of corridors, bedrooms, pantries, and toilet areas. Ten generations of pack rat may use the nest, extending it many times—a new rat (but only one) moving in on the demise of the previous owner until the debris in it may become an unnatural history of the area, a Collyer house in miniature.

The pack rat must outbreed his manifold enemies, and he keeps his numbers up, in favorable habitats, to about four animals to the acre. This can mean a fairly urgent sex life, up to three families raised every year. Young pack rats, fastened by notched teeth to their mother's teats, are not fazed or dislodged by copulation or bumpy sprints up trees as mama flees her en-

emies. A pack rat's split personality makes him neither careful nor quiet in his wanderings in a woods cabin —a favorite haunt—and he bumps around like an amiable Dr. Jekyll until everybody is awake. Then, at the first creak of a bedspring, he hammers his feet and scuttles like Mr. Hyde.

Is he, then, a rat fink, or just lovable? To find out, we corner him in our cabin. Trembling, he stands up abruptly, and now we know he is a squirrel. But no! Suddenly he has become a tiny kangaroo with his forepaws raised in a Jim Jeffries stance of resistance. He is going to punch the hell out of our ankles. But no; he backs up, still standing, still squaring off, whiskers blurred with movement. So cute! But schizophrenic to the end. We reach down and he either lets us catch him or, faster than the eye can follow, sinks his teeth into our hand and disappears.

But, we know one thing clearly. In two minutes or less he will be back, like an old friend, or enemy, for our transistor radio, our calendar watch, our gold signet ring, our electric toothbrush, our silver-trimmed comb, our miniature reading light, our wrist compass, our three-color ball-point pen . . .

But what were *we* doing with those things in the first place?

A New Zealander by birth, an American by adoption, Franklin Russell lives on a Jersey farm and writes about ecology.

DOES YOUR ROOM LOOK LIKE THE COLLYER BROTHERS'?

Every man should have a hobby—collecting stamps, say, and coins and shells and books and bottles and old newspapers and automobile parts and breadboxes and bedsprings and . . .

As I begin, I think of my cardboard boxes. There they are, crammed with the debris of a decade at least: children's drawings, aged desk calendars, a 1948 copy of *Life* with the stories of Truman's victory and the Donora smog, a guarantee for a vacuum cleaner as long defunct as the marriage it tidied up after, letters and bank statements, an old Army Air Corps surplus map of Borneo, and—why?—a photo-engraver's wood block with a picture of a gorilla. Don't be disdainful. You, too, have your piled attic, your "hell corner," your Fibber McGee closet ready to trip its booby-trap freight of old Muriel cigar boxes and baseball mitts with the Snuffy Sternweiss autograph imprint. We keep them, perhaps, because they are the closest representations that we have of ourselves: these are the things that have formed the shape of *our* time. And yet, there must be moments in our nightmares when the boxes seem to swell and we see ourselves engulfed by our own useless accumulations.

In the Harlem house of Homer and Langley Collyer we find the nightmare materialized. For three weeks twenty-two years ago, we all took inventory of its contents, truckload after truckload; by the time the last of the Collyers' effects had been carted away, the obsession of two old men had permanently entered our language and our mythic subconscious. For years my mother put it to me this way: "Aren't you ashamed? Your room looks like the Collyer brothers'."

The story broke on March 21, 1947.

At about ten that morning a call came in to police headquarters, and a male voice—no one ever satisfactorily established whose—announced, "There is a man dead in the premises at 2078 Fifth Avenue." Here, for almost forty years, had lived two legendary and mysterious recluses, Homer and Langley Collyer. Their doors were padlocked, their windows were boarded up; they had long ago cut off all gas, water, electricity, and sewer connections. Homer, paralyzed and, as *The New York Times* said, "blind as the poet he was named for," had rarely been seen since the 1930's; Langley, his younger brother, prowled the city at night, scrounging food—and collecting.

When the enigmatic call came on that morning in March, a patrolman was dispatched to the Collyer house. He found himself pounding at the front door of a weathered three-story brownstone on the northwest corner of Fifth Avenue and 128th Street. Getting no response, he summoned the emergency squad. With axes and crowbars they broke down the door and were confronted, the *Herald Tribune* reported, "with a wall of newspapers, folding chairs, broken boxes, part of a wine press, half a sewing machine, folding beds, parts of a rocking chair, and innumerable other pieces of junk." They tried the front basement door and again found their way barred by junk. It was the same at the back.

A policeman climbed up on a fire ladder to one of the second-floor windows. He could not even get a foot inside. By this time a crowd of some six hundred people had gathered below, and they gaped at the things that came hurtling out of the window: a rake . . . a baby carriage frame . . . the New York *Evening Telegram* for November 24, 1918 (REDS KILL 500 WHILE RUSSIANS FIGHT FOR FOOD). At last the patrolman disappeared from view, only to return to the window a few moments later.

"There's a D.O.A. here," he called down.

Behind a stinking mountain of junk the beam of his flashlight had fallen on the body of a tiny old man sitting on the floor. His matted hair reached down to his shoulders, and he wore only a ragged bathrobe. Next to the corpse were a half-eaten Washington State apple, a leaking container of rancid milk, and a copy of the Philadelphia *Jewish Morning Journal* of Sunday, February 22, 1920. Homer Collyer, it first appeared, had been dead at least ten hours, though that

By ROBERT COWLEY

estimate was later revised upward to from four days to a week; he had apparently succumbed to heart disease aggravated by starvation.

But what had become of Langley?

"That the collecting mania," writes A. A. Brill in *Fundamental Conceptions of Psychoanalysis*, "is a reaction to an unconscious need, to an inner feeling of voidness concerning some particular craving is best seen in the collections made by the insane." In the case of Langley and Homer Collyer we know of the void only through inference. They were born in New York in the 1880's and probably never left the city during their whole lives. Their father, Dr. Herman L. Collyer, was a prominent and wealthy gynecologist, a circumstance that seems noteworthy, since neither of his sons ever married or had, as far as is known, any contact with women. Their allegiances belonged all to their mother, a doting and possessive woman who was fond of reading the classics aloud to them in Greek. Homer went to the City College of New York, studied admiralty law, and practiced for a time. Langley majored in engineering at Columbia but never held a job. When the family moved into the 128th Street house, Harlem was a neighborhood favored by the white middle class. In the early 1900's Manhattan suffered one of its periodic real-estate collapses; Negroes began to migrate to Harlem, and a white exodus followed. But the Collyer brothers could never bring themselves to leave the Harlem house. It was as if their own fear kept them there, these two frail, genteel men with their fine old New York accents, barricading themselves against a world that was in every sense getting blacker and blacker.

Homer went blind and presently lost the use of his limbs as well. He refused to see a doctor—or was it that Langley would not let him? "You must remember we are the sons of a doctor," Langley said. "Homer eats 100 oranges a week—and is improving." Langley would appear after dark, a wraith in a greasy cloth cap, pulling a cardboard box on the end of a long rope. Sometimes he would walk as far as the Williamsburg section of Brooklyn for whole-wheat bread. As for the tons of newspapers in the house, he explained that he was saving them for the day when Homer regained his sight: "He can catch up on the news."

That was the only reason Langley ever gave for their collecting. "A passion for collecting is frequently a direct surrogate for a sexual desire," wrote the psychiatrist Karl Abraham, "and

in that case a delicate symbolism is often concealed, behind the choice of objects collected." But there is something monstrous about the Collyers that defies psychological explanation. One thinks of the police officer who, on a day in 1942, decided to check on a rumor that Homer was dead. After considerable hesitation, Langley let him in at the basement door and then led him up a pitch-black stairway through precarious canyons of newsprint, under alarm systems that would spew garbage and tin cans on the heads of the unwary and the uninvited—delicately poised booby traps that would bring down a suffocating edifice of junk. Did the policeman trip on the jawbone of the horse? Did he collide with the chassis of the Model T Ford or brush against the medical skeletons of the late Dr. Collyer? He found himself crawling on all fours through narrow, mazelike tunnels. It took him half an hour to reach the second-floor room, a small cleared section of which Homer inhabited.

"I switched on my flashlight," the policeman related, "and there was Homer sitting up like a mummy . . . 'I am Homer L. Collyer, lawyer,' the old man says, in a deep voice. 'I want your name and shield number. I am not dead. I am blind and paralyzed.'"

Some nights later Langley appeared at police headquarters to protest the invasion of privacy. It would be five years before anyone saw Homer again.

Homer was buried in the family plot in Queens, in the somber presence of the press and suddenly materialized relatives. The funeral was delayed in hopes that Langley would miraculously show up, but he did not. An eleven-state alarm was sent out. He was variously reported in Atlantic City, in Asbury Park, New Jersey, where policemen rummaged through boarded-up summer cottages, on a subway in Brooklyn, and floating in a creek in the east Bronx.

Meanwhile the clearing out of the house continued. In room after room junk was stacked to the ceiling, and Langley's alimentary burrows were the only way through. Nineteen tons were brought out one day . . . eighteen another . . . twelve tons, including five from a single six-foot area. By the time police and sanitation men were finished, 140 tons—280,000 thing-pounds —had been carted away.

Then, on April 8, nineteen days after the search had begun, a detective rooting not ten feet from where Homer had died looked down and saw a shoe. Langley Collyer had been crushed by one of his own booby traps as he carried food to his brother through a tunnel lined with a chest of drawers and an old bedspring. On the body—which could only be identified by the two suits and the striped overalls it was dressed in—there rested bundles of newspapers, a suitcase filled with metal, a sewing machine, and three breadboxes.

INDIAN GIVING

Being a treatise on the curious and exemplary custom of the potlatch: or how to kill your enemy with kindness, bankrupt your competitor with generosity, bury your mother-in-law with useless presents, and become poorer but richer by getting rid of everything

The problem, as every member of the acquisitive society will have noticed by now, is not in amassing things but in getting rid of them. Look into your closets, O Western World, and you will see a rising flood of things threatening to engulf you—a surfeit of all the fair and flagrant things that human and mechanical ingenuity can devise. One acquires them as desiderata; afterward, many of them turn out to be things that the department of sanitation cannot be prevailed upon to haul away. Sometimes, by happy chance, one can manage to lose things, and three moves are as good as a fire, as my New England grandmother used to say. But a far more stylish way of disposing of a lot of things in a hurry is the time-honored northwest-coast Indian potlatch. In the midst of our great crisis of the Malthusian supermarket a study of the ways of the potlatchers can teach us something.

The Indians of the Pacific coast used to be very good at making things, and they produced vast quantities of them, for they lived in a region where the salmon and halibut were so thick they did everything but catch themselves. That left the human population with time on their hands for making spruce-root rain hats, mountain-sheep horn spoons, cedarwood boxes inlaid with haliotis shell and snail opercula, argillite grease-dishes, maplewood soapberry-beating paddles, blankets of mountain-goat hair and cedar bark, whale's-tooth amulets, and such.

Since arts and crafts (and, to a lesser extent, sex) were the Indians' main pre-occupation before the white man introduced liquor, money, and bookkeeping, their longhouses would periodically fill to overflowing with the results of everybody's incessant basket weaving, wood carving, and stone chiseling. But to keep these from becoming a burden on the tribal psyche, their chief would hold a potlatch and give everything away in one great orgy of generosity. Potlatches were given to celebrate the accession of a new chief, the raising of a totem pole, the assumption of a crest or title, and so on; the word derives from the Nootka *patshatl*, "to give." If the potlatching chief impoverished himself and his clan in the process, so much the better, for by his very lavishness he acquired an unpurchasable esteem in the community. Besides, custom dictated that the recipients of his gifts must go him one better at their next potlatch.

A proper potlatch involved prodigious displays of eating, since it was a point of honor with the host to provide much more food than his guests could consume. The eating would last for days, interspersed with singing, belching, speechmaking, dramatic performances, and the ceremonial conferring of honorific names. But the vital part of the occasion was the bestowing of gifts—bowls, boxes, baskets, blankets, canoes, ornaments, sculptures—that the chief had collected among his people, from each according to his ability, and now distributed among his guests, to each according to his rank.

Potlatching replaced warfare and violence as a way of settling tribal dis-putes after the Canadian and United States governments began asserting their authority along the coast. "When I was young I saw a stream of blood shed in war," said an old Kwakiutl in a speech in 1895. "But since that time the white men came and stopped up that stream of blood with wealth. Now we fight with our wealth."

The Hudson's Bay Company's factory-made blankets replaced deerskin and mountain-goat robes just at the time when potlatching reached new heights of conspicuous consumption, having been accelerated by the tribal chiefs' need to assert their prerogatives in a rapidly changing world. A chief grown wealthy in the fur trade would demonstrate his contempt for property by giving away and destroying whole households—burning canoes, clubbing slaves to death, and breaking his most valuable "coppers" in the process. The coppers—shaped like shields and embossed with totemic figures—were, in effect, bills of high denomination that enabled a chief to get rid of a great deal of wealth at one go. Often they were worth more than their weight in gold, for they had the disconcerting habit of doubling their value every time they changed hands; and it was not uncommon for a copper to be worth ten or fifteen thousand trade blankets.

To be able to break so powerful a copper before an audience of one's invited rivals was a tremendous honor. But the game was usually rigged, since the broken pieces could be picked up and either resold at a profit or used to embarrass a neighbor. "A chief may

By FREDERIC V. GRUNFELD

break his copper and give the broken parts to his rival," explains the pioneer anthropologist Franz Boas, who watched a lot of potlatching before the turn of the century. "If the latter wants to keep his prestige, he must break a copper of equal or higher value, then return both his own broken copper and the fragments which he received . . ."

Later, when coppers went out of circulation, the potlatch people shifted to trade goods and introduced a whole department-store repertory to take their place. The Kwakiutl chief Daniel Cranmer drew up a partial inventory for the anthropologist Helen Codere when he described a memorable potlatch he held at Village Island, British Columbia, in 1921: "I gave him [the chief of nearby Cape Mudge village] a gas boat and $50 cash. Altogether that was worth $500 . . . The same day I gave Hudson's Bay blankets. I started giving out the property. First the canoes. Two pool tables were given to two chiefs. It hurt them. They said it was the same as breaking a copper. The pool tables were worth $350 apiece. Then bracelets, gas lights, violins, guitars were given to the more important people. Then 24 canoes, some of them big ones, and four gas boats." Later he handed out jewelry, shawls, sweaters, and shirts for women and young people; button blankets, shawls, and four hundred trade blankets; washtubs, teapots, cups, and about a thousand washbasins. Handfuls of small change were flung to the children. "The fourth day I gave away furniture: boxes, trunks, sewing machines, gramophones, bedsteads and bureaus. The fifth day I gave away cash. The sixth day I gave away about 1,000 sacks of flour worth $3 a sack. I also gave sugar." When it was over, he was unchallengeably one up on every other chief in the region. "All the chiefs say now in a gathering, 'You cannot expect that we can ever get up to you. You are a great mountain.'"

Potlatches of a sort are still given occasionally in the northwest-coast Indian country, but nowadays the institution retains only a faint glimmer of its former magnificence. Since they no longer have art objects to give away, they simply throw parties at which everybody receives . . . money. The end is clearly in sight. The white man has never shown much understanding for the potlatch; it was outlawed by the Canadian government, and even the most sympathetic anthropologists have described it as an "atrocious" and "paranoid" pursuit of social prestige. Most of them have missed the point; namely, that potlatching was essentially a primitive, preliterate form of investment banking.

From an economist's standpoint the wealthy Indian chief accomplished the same results by ostensibly giving things away as does the modern millionaire by supposedly holding on to them. In our paper economy the millionaire doesn't keep his wealth around the house, either—except for a Modigliani or two. What he doesn't need for his personal consumption he gives to a bank, in the form of pieces of power-paper inscribed with totems. The bank, in turn, ladles it out to the economy as a whole in the form of loans. The main thing is that people (beginning with the bank manager) must know that the money, though invisible, is actually there. It is this knowledge that determines a man's status as a millionaire; otherwise he's just a Collyer brother.

A Kwakiutl chief, depositing his wealth with his rivals, also depended on that public knowledge for his power, though he never had to worry about bankruptcies or a drop in the price of coppers. At the highest level, the cycle of acquisition and distribution is virtually identical in both cases. If our millionaire is very, very rich, social pressure and the tax structure will induce him, sooner or later, to do some heavy potlatching of the modern sort: the name of the game is Rockefeller Foundation.

Frederic V. Grunfeld lives on the island of Majorca, where he makes sheep-horn spoons to give away in his free time.

GARBAGE, OR, CAN WE EVER GET AWAY FROM IT ALL?

A famous Soviet leader once promised to bury us, but we are achieving the goal without his help

On a narrow strip of Jersey marsh, garbage men are building a land bank; it grows day by day, stretching always a little farther from the black, polluted waters of Newark Bay toward its final limit: the edge of a six-lane interstate highway. At any hour, one can watch at least thirty sanitation trucks making their way across the top of the new bank. The covered trucks follow rutted roadways built from loads of broken brick and concrete that have been set aside from the flimsier trash, garbage, and household refuse. The trucks rock slowly up and down over the ruts, like heavy work-boats pitching in an oily sea, as they head for the open face of the bank, the slope on which loads are currently dumped. In fifteen years, more than a thousand acres have been covered with waste twelve feet deep from the cities of northern New Jersey. The speed of covering continually increases, both because the population of north Jersey is growing and because every American discards more waste each year.

New Jersey is one of the few states with strict regulations governing the operation of sanitary landfills. The proprietors of this marshland site must cover the dumped material with clean soil six inches deep, leaving only one day's working surface open and uncovered, to a limit of 15,000 square feet. Following the trucks out to the working face, one meets the smell of refuse only when one approaches that uncovered space, where five Caterpillars rumble back and forth over recent dumping, compacting the fill and spreading the dirt that lies in piles on the already completed surface. When the smell comes, it is not the heart-stopping stench of sewage and animal decay but the stale, dusty odor of trash and chemicals, sweetened by only an intermittent whiff of the sickly scent of wet garbage. Papers that have blown loose from the heavier material before the dirt can be pushed over it dart fitfully across the landscape. They provide the only sign of life: the papers and the birds. Small bands of starlings, stubby creatures, peck at scraps of food caught in the soil cover; they are ignored by the great crowd of sea gulls. A few of the gulls work their way up into the sky on heavy wingbeats, to glide there, high above the emptying trucks; thousands squat near the trucks on a layer of fill already discovered, waiting for news of sudden riches from the air-borne birds above.

Across the highway from the fill a great international airport spreads one runway parallel to the road. One herring gull, beating upward across the nose of a climbing airliner, can be sucked into one of the plane's mammoth jet pods where, dying, it may snuff out a hundred lives in a thunderous catastrophe. The public authority that owns the airport has shown its uneasiness over the proximity of gulls to jet planes, but no government has clear, final power to determine how great the danger is or what should be done about it. The question hovers over the landfill rather like the gulls themselves.

The strange possibility that buried refuse can reach up from the ground, as it were, to snatch an airliner from the sky, symbolically suggests the complex scope of industrial man's unprecedented need to shed the substances he has used but no longer wants. When men were farmers the problem was simpler; they threw away what they could not eat, and patched, mended, spliced, and sewed their other possessions forever. Industrial society discards a flood of objects so torrential that it may well drown us. Each year, in the United States, the trash contains a smaller and smaller portion of organic residues, which gradually change into humus, and a bigger and bigger portion of change-resistant, man-made artifacts and potions: old machines and their parts, bits of cities knocked down or dug up to be discarded, plastic containers in which men deliver their goods to one another, useless when emptied, tubs of chemicals that have served their purpose and represent the now-worthless distillate of vast quantities of raw materials extracted from the earth.

For an added irony, consider that the attempt to salvage useful flotsam from the flood founders on the very productivity that originally created it. A system capable of producing eight million automobiles a year must run smoothly; it cannot be slowed down to adjust to the slight irregularity in its operation that re-used components might cause. A labor force that is paid enough to buy back its produce cannot be put to work digging for valuable sherds in the wrack of last year's me-

By ROGER STARR

chanical marvels, or yesterday's.

A calm marble statue with missing head and arms may well be the supreme symbol of the Greek desire to achieve order and moderation in a turbulent world. The descriptive modern artifact may well be the automobile hulk with shattered windows and missing wheels, the object of supreme romantic love reduced to a cause for mere embarrassment in only ten years.

Everyone remembers the glowing pride that suffused the family lined up along its driveway as Dad arrived from the dealer's in his new car; we reeled at the fresh scent of the synthetic leather, a perfume that vanished almost as quickly as the glow of a martini. The new car's glory is so brief that the first fender dent affects us like the clap of doom. How evanescent our life is! In the movie *Goldfinger* violent death for hundreds of male and female agents evoked not a quiver from the audiences, but the premature pressing of a mint-new Lincoln Continental into a block of scrap metal brought gasps of horror. By the time Dad turns into his driveway for the first time, his car has lost perhaps one-third of its value. Within a year it is no longer even thought of as new; within ten years it has become completely valueless. Some of its components—the wheels and tires, for example—may bring a few pennies from a scrap dealer, but not enough to pay anyone to remove them. The body is virtually worthless at the moment of its obsequies, even though it still holds several electric motors, intricately machined pistons and gears, laminated safety glass, to mention only a few bits of junk that could not have been purchased for an emperor's treasure only a hundred years ago. They will be buried now under twelve feet of other trash, there to remain until some day when, the relative values of labor and natural resources having changed, they will be dug up to provide raw materials for no-one-knows-what new artifacts to please no-one-knows-how-many hundreds of millions of men and women,

who will then be discarding no-one-knows-what miraculous products not yet invented, until the globe—unless already terminated for some other reason—will consist only of a mass of discarded material in which all the elements needed to sustain organic life will be locked in a permanent but sterile chemical embrace. But automobiles—Americans throw away more than four million of them a year—are only a small part of America's garbage heaps. No figures are readily available to indicate the number of refrigerators and other major mechanical appliances discarded each year, but these, too, constitute a tremendous total of technical complexity, weight and bulk.

A visit to a landfill operation, or a drive through the streets of an American city during "Clean-up Week"—an annual period in some cities when residents are permitted to discard without penalty *any* object, however large, for disposal by the sanitation department or sanitary contractors—will quickly indicate that Americans also throw away sofas, mattresses, lamps, bent gutters and leaders from their houses, jarfuls of flammable paint thinners and cleaning fluids, and broken clocks, radios, television sets. During clean-up week these objects are piled on the curbs, a melancholy fringe along the trimmed edges of suburbia.

And then there is the simple daily disgorging of soda-pop bottles, soup cans, cardboard and plastic containers, orange peels. Statisticians estimate that the average American home produces four and a half pounds of solid waste per person per day, more by far than any other nation.

This rough tally of identifiable municipal wastes has skipped the anonymous commercial and industrial waste products that constitute the largest single segment of the disposable tonnage: vast quantities of fly ash, the residue of pulverized coal that has been burned under electric generating-station boilers; debris from construction and demolition sites; by-product chem-

icals perhaps too degraded for any commerical re-use, but flammable nonetheless and hence a nuisance in a sanitary landfill; restaurant garbage; rock and dirt dug up from excavation sites within the city.

Modern man can no longer avoid the consequences of his own productivity: all these things must be put *somewhere*. Almost every city in the nation is embroiled in some sort of controversy over the final disposition of its own waste, but the vigor of the arguments cannot stretch the possibilities for disposal. There remain only four possibilities on this planet, if one dismisses the likelihood of shooting the earthly waste out into space. Of the four the most sanguine hope is that waste can be reclaimed for future use. Hardly a month passes without a happy announcement that someone has developed a method for turning garbage into topsoil, or mining it for small quantities of rich metals like gold and silver. So far no reclaiming system has proved economically attractive to American mayors, under the local ground rules that govern this subject. This comes as bad news to those who remember that when they pulled K.P. in the army they were expected to divide wastes carefully into separate cans, presumably to facilitate the re-use of fats for explosives, paper products for new paper manufacture, and bones for chemicals and soap. The army system depended upon the availability of low-paid and underemployed laborers with a plethora of sergeants aching to keep their charges busy.

When reclamation is not feasible, some solid wastes can be disposed of in the air. They need only to be combined with oxygen; that is to say, burned. Large-scale municipal incinerators can, in theory, be designed to operate with great efficiency at very high temperatures. Such incinerators would not at all resemble the messy steel wigwams, now in use in many dumps, that merely create a slightly improved draft in a smelly bonfire. Since paper and paper products constitute almost half of present solid waste, a large, efficient furnace could be designed to burn this material at a temperature of 3,000 degrees Fahrenheit. Such a furnace would require no other fuel than the combustibles contained in the waste. It could actually generate enough heat to serve some useful purpose, perhaps making steam to warm nearby apartments. An efficient incinerator produces neither smoke nor odor, but it is costly to build and requires expert supervision and maintenance.

Even the most efficient and smoke-free incinerator, however, creates an invisible residue in the form of carbon-dioxide gas, the result of combustion. If all the solid wastes in the world were burned daily, a considerable quantity of carbon dioxide would be added to the volumes already produced today by the combustion of fossil fuels like coal and oil. Does this matter to anyone? The question is less easily answered than framed. But as the rate of combustion increases and, coincidentally, as the stands of forest and other plant life throughout the world decrease, the measurable carbon dioxide content of the atmosphere is increasing. Clearly the maintenance of the oxygen–carbon-dioxide balance is vital to all forms of life on this planet. Would large-scale, efficient incineration of waste affect this balance? Nobody quite knows.

If depositing wastes in the air, even under the best possible circumstances, raises questions that no one can answer, what about stowing wastes on the land? This possibility raises a different question: which land shall be used? Traditionally, municipal sanitation commissioners and private landfill operators have chosen swamps or marshes for their landfill operations. No one particularly wanted the wetlands. The very word swamp suggests uselessness. It is easy enough to convince the governing body of a city that the fill will simply be making a beautiful golf course out of a mosquito incubator. Landfill operations designed

only to hide waste have not been the only consumers of wetlands, which have also disappeared to create land for housing developments, highways, and harbors. But garbage disposal is a relentless need that cannot be long deferred. Only recently has anyone begun to notice how much coastline has been changed to make room for garbage. Connecticut, for example, watched more than half its wetlands disappear before the state passed a law that lends them a measure of protection against bulkheading and fill.

Marine and ornithological biologists have been able to establish that wetlands breed far more than mosquitoes; in fact the tidal marshlands produce more usable protein per acre than the richest farm land in the world. The protein, however, is not consumed directly by men and women, an unfortunate accident, for the small aquatic animals that do consume it are not represented in the state legislatures or Congress. These small creatures are in turn eaten by shellfish or the fry of important fish, including menhaden, winter flounder, and striped bass. Decline in the productivity of offshore fisheries can be traced to the obliteration of coastal marshes, not only because the nutrients for young fish disappear, but also due to the disappearance of the small coastal watercourses in which

pelagic fish spawn and are hatched. Unfortunately, fishermen who depend on the fish population for their livelihood have only recently gained the sophistication to add their voice to those of the conservationists.

Fresh-water wetlands, also popular for landfill, are not the nuisances they have generally been taken for. They are natural sumps, gathering rainfall that penetrates the substrata of the land and keeps the water table constant. It is ironic that in some areas, Long Island for one, where natural fresh-water wetlands have been filled in for housing sites, artificial sumps have had to be dug to replace the hydrologic function. There are in many parts of the country far more suitable barren areas, productive of little wildlife, that could be used effectively for depositing solid waste if the filling operation were intelligently handled and carefully controlled. There are many big holes in America—the holes of vast mining operations—that could be filled successfully with solid wastes to everyone's benefit, but few municipalities are ready to spend the money to transport their wastes to the places where they would be welcome. Solid wastes, moving to these mines, may someday be the most dependable bulk cargo of the railroads. Used properly, these wastes can even create attractive sur-

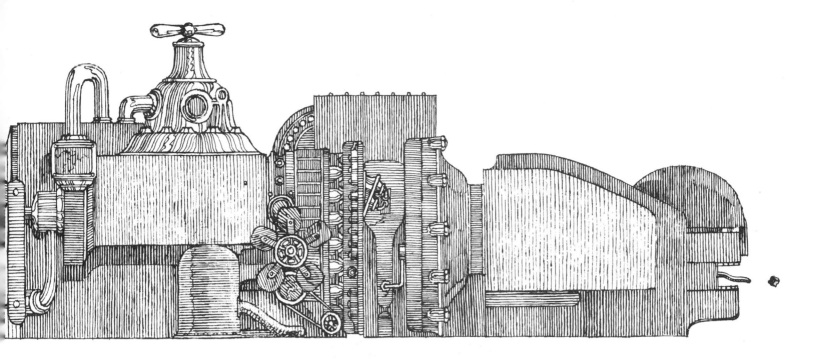

roundings. In the vicinity of Chicago a combination of waste and excavated material has been used to build up a hill that is now used as a ski slope. Its stability indicates that compacted fill, placed intelligently, can modify flat land and turn it into interesting landscape with unexpected recreational uses.

If the uses of land are limited, the only remaining depository is the water. But here the courts have raised a cautious hand. The Supreme Court has held that wastes cannot be simply dumped into the ocean, for no government in the United States has the right to inflict a nuisance on the beaches of its neighbors. Too much of the solid waste load floats. The key to the constructive use of water as a final disposal site for solid waste lies in the compaction of the waste to increase its specific gravity. The Japanese have developed a press capable of compacting solid waste so tightly that it will not disintegrate. The compaction raises the specific gravity so high that the material sinks like a rock. These bundles, dumped at sea, would simply settle on the bottom, where they would not harm anything and might form artificial reefs that would be of help to the fish population. Land for unwelcome uses—monster jetports, for example—might be constructed from bundles of supercompacted waste, which would

save precious wetlands and the ears and nerves of those living nearby.

Ultimately it becomes clear that our planet is limited, like any house, and that the time will come when its attic will overflow with the accumulated debris of years of habitation. There is the difference, however, that when the attic of a house fills up, one may clean it out and pay someone to take the debris away. But things cannot be carted away from the earth; our planet, as the economist Kenneth Boulding has told us, is a spaceship to which nothing can be added and from which nothing can be taken away. The ultimate problem of solid waste is not that the waste itself takes up valuable room on the spaceship but that the stock of elements is limited, and if the elements are locked into waste irretrievably, they are lost to human life. As the character of man's waste has changed—from organic compounds capable of decomposition and regeneration through the metabolic processes of life, to compounds such as plastics, which resist decomposition—so the ability of the earth to sustain life may have been impaired. It is quite possible that at some time or other so much of the needed life matter will be locked into waste that the earth will not be able to sustain the population living on it. One assumes that the earth will reach this

tipping point slowly, after a long period during which raw materials will become scarcer and more expensive, the standard of living will decline, and the quality of the natural environment deteriorate. And one assumes that given warning, mankind will do something to stave off disaster.

But even with ample warning there is little to suggest that men will be able to change direction. At stake here is man's ability, nay willingness, to control his own productivity, to measure the seriousness of the waste that will result from each extension of his productivity, each new artifact, each new human life. The control over inventiveness, love, and hunger that would be required in order to utilize natural resources wisely and avoid crossing the balance point might well destroy so many of the human values that man would be incapable of asserting this control. Will men prefer to drown in the waste of their pleasures? Or will they prefer to control them in the hope of prolonging life? This, nothing less, is the question that lies burning at the bottom of the dump.

Part of Roger Starr's garbage underlies an enlarged Longshore Country Club near his home in Westport, Connecticut. And he is now helping to fill an unsightly mud-flat area near the Saugatuck River.

51

THE MANY FACES OF KARL MARX

Prophet, historian, newspaperman, revolutionary, philosopher, fond papa—all these faces were his, and one other: the romantic idealist exhorting man to triumph over the things he manufactures

One can imagine few greater shocks to our sense of the fitness of things than a revelation that Karl Marx without his beard had the face of a romantic poet, another Byron or Shelley. We are used to seeing him in the guise of an angry prophet, beard bristling with outrage at the iniquities of his opponents; or nobly marmoreal in profile, with a similar profile of Engels or Lenin apparently adhering to one of his ears, as one sees them on innumerable communist posters. The beards of the saints of European communism seem a part of their roles: Marx's leonine and denunciatory; Engels's brisk and worldly; Lenin's a jutting icebreaker, forging forward toward the happy land over the always-receding horizon.

Yet the suggestion that the young Marx might have had a face of dreamy, romantic sensitivity—though literally speaking highly improbable, to judge from the clues among the bristles—is not altogether symbolically inappropriate. Marx was an idealistic young man, born into a romantic environment, whose early ardors bear unmistakably the marks of a youth of the generation of Hector Berlioz and Victor Hugo, a generation to which Byron and Napoleon, Prometheus and Faust, were the symbols of their own thwarted aspirations, pent up by the stuffy reaction that gripped Europe in the years after Waterloo. To many of that generation "revolution" was a holy word, and the spirit of freedom appeared, as in Delacroix's famous painting, as a beautiful bare-breasted woman leading the workers at the barricades. The years of Marx's youth and early man-

hood were the years before the European revolutions of 1848, when it seemed that with one final titanic effort humanity might throw off all its oppressors at one blow and create from the ashes of the old social order a new world of justice and freedom. Paris was revered by young men as the holy city of revolution. As the Russian socialist Aleksandr Herzen put it, "I entered the city with reverence, as men used to enter Jerusalem or Rome."

The fate of captive countries like Italy and Poland, ruled by oppressor nations whose domination had been reaffirmed at the Congress of Vienna, touched liberal consciences as Spain was to do in the 1930's and Hungary in the 1950's. Not only proletarians but artists and intellectuals of all kinds felt, during these years, the revolutionary itch; when revolution came to Europe's capitals in 1848–49, they went with the workers to the barricades.

It was to this generation that Karl Marx, born in 1818, belonged. There is

no cause for surprise that he became a revolutionary; it would almost have been surprising if he had not. What distinguished him from most of his contemporaries was that in Marx youthful fervor soon became transmuted into scientific rigor, without abating its revolutionary character. Marx's revolutionary zeal thus acquired a staying power, while that of most of his contemporaries—vaguer, more hazily idealistic—faded with age and disillusionment. Nevertheless, Marx's "scientific" socialism never altogether lost a visionary, apocalyptic aureole that occasionally gives a lurid glow to the gray pages of *Capital* and recalls the ardent years before the false dawn of 1848. In his personal tastes, too, Marx remained a man of his generation; he shared that passionate love of Shakespeare that struck the intellectual youth of France and Germany in the early nineteenth century with the force of a revelation; for him, too, Prometheus, the archetypal rebel, the Titan who had defied Zeus, was a potent symbol, as he was for Shelley, Goethe, and Beethoven. Marx's taste in novels, again, was not chiefly for realistic novels of industrial England or Flaubert's brutal dissection of the French bourgeoisie, but for Sir Walter Scott and Alexandre Dumas the elder. Karl Marx, economist and visionary, German scholar and international revolutionary, contemptuous as he was of revolutionary phrasemakers and conspiratorial play-acting, was yet himself a powerful rhetorician and prophet of doom and regeneration, a romantic realist, a man of many faces.

By J. W. BURROW

The paradoxes begin with his birth. He was born of comfortably-off middle-class parents, not in one of the great centers of population and industry whose portentousness for the future he was so vehemently to proclaim, but in the ancient city of Trier. Marx was to experience poverty, but after, not before, he became a revolutionary. He never gained the firsthand experience of factory conditions possessed by his partner Friedrich Engels, the son of a Bremen manufacturer. Trier is a city of ancient monuments, set among the castle-dotted, vine-clustered terraces of the Moselle valley, only a few miles from the Luxembourg border and the forest of Ardennes. In one respect only was it an apt birthplace for Karl Marx. Trier, or Treves, which at the time of Marx's birth formed an outlying part of the dominions of the king of Prussia, had once been the gateway between the Latin and the Teutonic worlds; the great gate that marked the limits of the power of imperial Rome still stands, like a grandiose, abandoned Checkpoint Charlie, in the midst of Trier's traffic, a suitable reminder of a German who was also a cosmopolitan, to whom Paris and London were not only homes but the focus of his thoughts as the breeding grounds of revolution, a man who looked always to the West and has been honored in the East.

Marx's dreams were imperial in scale, ecumenical in scope, and grounded on a panoramic view of world history. Such cosmopolitanism, too, is characteristic of his generation. The French Revolution, the great beacon, extinguished yet still smoldering in the minds of men, especially of those too young to remember it, had been an ecumenical event; the fall of the Bastille, of little importance in itself, became a universal symbol, welcomed as eagerly in Britain and in Germany as in France itself. The nineteenth century is the classic age of the émigré intellectual, the cosmopolitan revolutionary, and the ideological *condottiere* fighting in a foreign land because liberty is every man's cause or because

the proletariat has no fatherland. Besides the prototype, Byron, there were Mickiewicz, Polish poet and professor at the Collège de France, who raised a Polish legion in 1848 to fight for Italian independence against the Austrians; the Russian anarchist-nobleman Bakunin, later to be Marx's archenemy in the First Workers' International, organzing revolt among the artisans of the Jura and leading the Saxon workers at the Dresden barricades; and the aged Garibaldi, leading an irregular and somewhat undisciplined column of volunteers against the Prussians in 1870 on behalf of the newly reborn French Republic. When Friedrich Engels and a handful of fellow communists stood by the graveside of Karl Marx in Highgate cemetery, London, in 1883, they were honoring one of the last, as well as one of the most intransigent and least fraternal, of that unofficial fraternity of revolt, dating from the days when romanticism and revolution were almost synonymous terms. The earliest, Byron, had died at Missolonghi nearly sixty years before. Engels at Marx's graveside acclaimed him as the man who had made socialism "scientific," but to the young Marx as a scholar in Germany forty years earlier, politics had come first in a different guise, through the medium of philosophy and the romantic rhetoric of the emancipation of the human spirit.

In his secure niche in the placid, comely, preindustrial world of Trier and the German university towns, it was not personal oppression or the sight of proletarian misery and industrial squalor that first turned Marx into a revolutionary, but the enthusiasms of his generation and the theories of his elders, the intellectual diet he encountered as a student, on which young Germany was eagerly feeding. Marx the philosopher and the romantic humanist preceded Marx the politician and Marx the anatomist of industrial society. The philosophy Marx imbibed at the universities of Bonn and Berlin taught that man is truly himself, truly human, only when his activities are

willed by himself, when he is not manipulated by others, by blind forces, or brute *things* as a mere object, only when he chooses, rationally, to act as his own human essence dictates. The young Marx, applying this philosophy with his own uncompromising rigor, came to the conclusion that however free men might be in the abstract, legally speaking, as workers the majority were not free at all. Labor was, or should be, the highest expression of humanity, the activity by which men freely shaped and changed the world, subjecting *things* to the creative power of man. But labor, the essence of man's humanity, his godlike creative power, had itself been degraded into a thing and was bought and sold as a commodity. Instead of productive labor being used by humanity, human beings were used to produce products. The workers, the proletariat, were not free in practice, whatever the law said. The State was not their state, nor was it impartial, because it upheld the domination of the property owners. Man could only be free if labor was an assertion of men's own wills and creative power, rather than a commodity that they were forced to barter for wages, and this could only happen by the proletariat overthrowing the existing property relations and creating a state of real, as distinct from merely abstract, legal, freedom. As Marx wrote at this time: "Philosophy finds in the proletariat its material weapons." Marx the philosopher had become Marx the revolutionary politician.

He had also become a radical journalist, and it was this that led to his first self-enforced exile, to Paris and Brussels. In Paris Marx, now a committed socialist, saw for the first time the visible reality of the urban proletariat—which he had invoked as the savior of society—on a far larger scale than anything Germany could yet show. There, too, he found groups of other socialists. He learned from them, particularly from their critiques of capitalist economics; but chiefly it was in his intellectual struggles with them, his attempts to define his own position as a way of repudiating what he saw as the mistakes and eccentricities of theirs, that the "Marxism" of the *Communist Manifesto*, published in 1848, was born. The historian and social scientist was taking over from the idealistic philosopher of freedom.

The *Communist Manifesto* differs from most political pamphlets precisely in the breadth and grandeur of its historical perspective. The message is that history both promises victory and imposes conditions. From the ringing opening ("The history of all hitherto-existing society is the history of class struggles") to the final celebrated call to action ("The proletarians have nothing to lose but their chains. They have a world to win. Working men of all countries, unite!"), the idea is hammered home that capitalism is not the permanent state of mankind but simply the latest phase of historical development. The bourgeoisie is not respectable and law-abiding; it is dynamic and rapacious; it has won its way to power by smashing the ancient privileged regime of feudalism. Seldom has a political movement received such a gift as the *Manifesto*: at once an indictment, an analysis, and a promise of victory. Marx and his collaborator Engels, in the *Communist Manifesto*, join Jean Jacques Rousseau and Abraham Lincoln among the rare few who have given to a political attitude a classic rhetorical form. Like Magna Carta and the Declaration of Independence, the *Manifesto*, especially in its concluding sentences, has the resonance and power of myth; like *The Social Contract* and the Gettysburg Address, it gives definitive form to a hunger of the human spirit.

In the short run the prophecy was false, nor has the ensuing century done much to make it valid. The specter of communism, which Marx and Engels had declared to be haunting Europe, proved in 1848, not for the last time, to be a wraith. The masses in France, enfranchised by the new Republican government, voted overwhelmingly for property and order; the resistance of the Parisian workers was trampled into the gutters of the capital by the government's cavalry, and Marx, doubly exiled now that he had made France too hot for himself, arrived penniless in London, the grimy citadel of capitalism itself, where he was to spend the rest of his life. For Marx the would-be man of action the best years of his life were already behind him; the years of patient research had begun. Here in London he was to work, mole-like, dogged by poverty, exasperated by the political moderation of the English working class, laboriously documenting his thesis of the inevitable downfall of capitalism, adding to the philosophy of human emancipation and to the incandescent rhetoric of the *Communist Manifesto* the technical apparatus of economic analysis, the patiently accumulated facts of a massive indictment of a whole social system, and detailed analyses of the failure of the recent revolutions on the Continent.

It is the last that, together with the economic sections of *Capital*, establishes Marx as a great historian—probably, in terms of sheer intellectual power and penetration, the greatest historian of the nineteenth century, an author to whom modern historians, no matter how hard they try, can scarcely avoid being indebted. His most masterly work of detailed history, a study of the rise to power of the new French emperor, Napoleon III, by a *coup d'état* over the ruins of the short-lived Republic established in 1848, is only an extended essay, yet it contains a revolution in the writing of history. Using the concept of a socioeconomic class not merely as part of a political indictment but as a tool of historical explanation, Marx provides what is still the most penetrating and stimulating analysis of the character and the success of Napoleon III and also gives the classic account of the situation of the fascist dictator who claims to be "above" class and politics and to represent symbolically the unity of the nation.

Marx's essay is outstanding for the subtlety and minuteness with which he lays bare the ironies of history and the intricacies, the agitated twists and turns, of the various sections of French society, particularly the French bourgeoisie; parodying its cult of "order," Marx represents it as capitulating to Napoleon III by its bleating: "Only theft can still save property; only perjury, religion; bastardy [Louis Napoleon's legitimacy was doubtful], the family; disorder, order!" Marx's contempt is tellingly balanced by the glimpses he gives of the perspectives of world history; they are, in a sense, his justification for treating Napoleon's regime as a comic masquerade. The spectacle of the great Napoleon's nephew stepping into his uncle's boots offered opportunities that Marx was not the man to miss. The note is struck in the first sentence: "Hegel remarks somewhere that all facts and personages of great importance in world history occur, as it were, twice. He forgot to add: the first time as tragedy, the second as farce." This tone, sometimes of polished irony, sometimes sheer vaudeville, is maintained throughout. As an example of the first, take Marx's dismissal of French liberals' excuses for Napoleon III's success: "It is not enough to say, as the French do, that their nation was taken unawares. A nation and a woman are not forgiven the unguarded hour in which the first adventurer that came along could violate them."

The essay on Louis Napoleon is not only the work of a profound and original historical and sociological intelligence; it also has the verve and impact of first-class journalism. It was a talent Marx was to need in his exile, not merely as a political weapon but as a means of staying alive. One of the many ironies in Marx's career is that he quarried his indictment of capitalism from the British government's reports in the scholarly security of the British Museum Reading Room, but another is that in the 1850's he saved himself and his family from destitution partly by becoming the respected London correspondent of the New York *Tribune*. The managing editor, Charles Anderson Dana, had met Marx in Germany when the latter was winning notoriety as the crusading editor of the *Neue Rheinische Zeitung*. After Marx fled to London, Dana asked him for regular articles, at five dollars apiece. At first Engels wrote them for him, but when Marx's English improved he took heart from Engels's declaration that the *Tribune*'s own English was appalling and began to write them himself. Fortunately Marx's attitude toward British imperialism and the British governing class was pretty much the same as that of his American employers, and the relationship was a moderately harmonious one.

The meager pay of the New York *Tribune* and the subsidies of Engels enabled Marx and his family to survive the first bitter years of exile in London. Turned out of their first lodgings into the street because of a mix-up over the rent, the family settled in two small rooms at 28 Dean Street, Soho Square, in a poor exiles' quarter, where the house is now surrounded by restaurants and strip-clubs. There they endured the hardships of genteel poverty. Marx wrote to Engels in 1852: "For a week past I have been in the pleasant position of being unable either to go out for want of my overcoats, which are at the pawnshop, or to eat meat because the butcher has stopped credit. The only good news we have here comes from my sister-in-law, the minister's wife, who announces that my wife's uncle is ill at last." In these circumstances, most witnesses agreed the Marx family created something very like a domestic idyll. Of the many faces of Karl Marx not the least surprising or remarkable is Marx the family man, a devoted husband, a jovial and indulgent father.

In 1843 Marx had married Jenny von Westphalen, the beautiful daughter of a neighbor in Trier, a Prussian government official. When they came to London, there were already three children, Jenny, Laura, and Edgar. Shortly after their arrival Guido was born and inevitably was nicknamed Fawkes, after the would-be dynamiter of the British Houses of Parliament; Marx's own nicknames were "the Moor"—a reference to his dark hair—and "Old Nick." Two more daughters, Franziska and Eleanor, were born later. The household was completed by "Lenchen," the Westphalens' family servant, who was said to be the only person who could subdue Marx. There may have been a reason for this. There were rumors at the time that Marx or Engels was the father of Lenchen's illegitimate son Frederick, and sub-

sequent evidence points to Marx. Whether this was the result of an isolated lapse from fidelity to Jenny or of a protracted liaison, we do not know.

Details of the Marx's family life are preserved by another exile and a disciple, Wilhelm Liebknecht, in a series of descriptive scenes that have the slightly comic naïveté of the sentimental paintings of domestic scenes of the period so beloved by the nineteenth-century bourgeoisie: pictures of a benign Marx patting urchins' heads like a Mr. Pickwick and giving them pennies and apples, or of the family picnics on Hampstead Heath. Liebknecht, who was obviously often hungry, recalled with particular tenderness a "substantial joint of roast veal . . . consecrated by tradition for the Sunday outings to Hampstead Heath. A basket of a size quite unusual in London, brought by Lenchen from Trier, was the tabernacle in which the holy of holies was borne. . . . Bread and cheese could be bought on the heath, where crockery, hot water and milk were also to be had, just as in a Berlin *Kaffeegarten*." After lunch the adults would sleep on the grass, read the Sunday papers, or give piggyback rides to the children, Marx being, according to his daughter Eleanor, a splendid horse. On the walk home they would sing German folk songs, or Marx would recite Shakespeare or Dante from memory.

Three of the children died, Guido and Franziska before reaching their first birthdays, so that Marx was especially agonized by the death of Edgar at the age of nine. To his daughters he was an indulgent and fascinating companion, joining in their horseplay and telling fantastic stories in the manner of E. T. A. Hoffmann. To his daughter Eleanor he was "the cheeriest, gayest soul that ever breathed . . . a man brimming over with humor and good humor, whose hearty laugh was infectious and irresistible . . . the kindliest, gentlest, most sympathetic of companions. . . . His kindness and patience were really sublime."

Marx's political opponents would have been intensely surprised to hear it. They knew Marx in another of his incarnations, as a practical politician, a man of domineering temper, brutal speech, and implacable rancor. His opponents were, of course, not only the bourgeoisie, which was virtually unaware of his existence, but his fellow socialists. Many of Marx's key works are polemics against the errors of some erstwhile comrade. A long succession of socialist theorists and leaders felt the edge of Marx's scorn and the crushing weight of his erudition as he fought them for control of the socialist parties and movements to which he at various times belonged. Marx was a formidable political opponent, but he had no conception of consensus politics; again and again he showed himself ready to abandon or wreck a promising movement rather than allow it to fall into the hands of those he regarded as doctrinally in error. His deliberate destruction of the First Workers' International to save it from the Russian anarchist Bakunin and his followers was only the most notable of these fatal self-administered purges.

Marx's irritability was no doubt exasperated by persistent ill health. When writing *Capital* he was severely troubled with hemorrhoids. As he wrote plaintively to Engels, "to finish I must at least be able to *sit down*," adding grimly, "I hope the bourgeoisie will remember my carbuncles." Utterly dedicated to the idea of revolution, Marx spent his life as an exile, despite his attempts to organize the German exiles and to collaborate with English working-class leaders, essentially as a scholar. He would have nothing to do with merely conspiratorial politics; there was no substitute for the travail of history and the political education of the workers by the class struggle. Marx's rejection of conspiracy was not due to moral objections or to natural coolness of temperament, but to a massive intellectual self-restraint, a contempt for impractical revolutionary dreaming and frothy oratory. He was in fact a man in whose nature aggression and revolt ran deep. In a questionnaire composed by his daughter Laura he once gave the answers: "Your idea of happiness. *To fight*; The vice you detest most. *Servility*; Favorite hero. *Spartacus, Kepler.*"

The official name of Marx's circle was the German Workers' Educational Society, and the educational aspect was taken seriously even when it had nothing to do with politics. Marx in this context wears the face of the German *Gelehrter*, with all the strengths and weaknesses of the type. There was nothing narrow about his intellectual interests. He could read all the main European languages and taught himself Russian when he was in his fifties. He read Greek and regularly reread Aeschylus. He was interested in the natural sciences and, of course, tech-

nology; he acclaimed Darwin and became highly excited when he saw a model of an electric train engine in a shop window. For relaxation he would do mathematics; during his wife's last illness he could find solace only in working on calculus. In his dealings with his young followers one sees not only Marx the political doctrinaire but also, more surprisingly, Marx the pedagogue. On the whole the latter sounds a good deal more intimidating: "How he scolded me one day," Liebknecht lamented, "because I did not know—Spanish! . . . Every day I was questioned and had to translate a passage from *Don Quixote*. . . ." Educational bullying was obviously part of Marx's nature, even apart from politics, and one can see in these reminiscences the professor he at one time seemed destined to become.

But ultimately, of course, the politician and social scientist were uppermost. Marx had already, before he came to London, developed his characteristic theory of history: that a society's legal and political institutions are an expression of its economic substructure. But it was in England, in the British Museum, that Marx did his fundamental research as an economist and social scientist and prepared his most celebrated work, *Capital*. Marx's book is a strange amalgam: it is a highly abstract theoretical economic analysis designed to show that the capitalist annexed all the surplus value produced by the worker, leaving the latter nothing but his bare subsistence, and himself contributing nothing; there is a good deal of detailed economic history, of which Marx was a pioneer, analyzing the earlier stages of capital accumulation, the dispossession of the European peasantry, and the development of European industrial and mercantile civilization. And there is the statistical demonstration of the human cost of early industrialism, compiled chiefly from the evidence of the British government's own commissions and the reports of its factory inspectors.

Marx here joins Dickens, Disraeli, Carlyle, and other Victorians appalled by the conditions of industrial and urban life. These pages of *Capital* are, for all Marx's attempts to refrain from mere denunciation, the work of an angry moralist who could see in the cold figures "the motley crowd of workers of all ages, and sexes, that press on us more insistently than did the souls of the slain on Ulysses."

Finally there is prophecy, deduced from a model of capitalist competition and production—intended to show the inevitability of increasingly frequent and disastrous economic crises and the ultimate revolt of the masses. In the *Communist Manifesto* Marx had called for this revolt and predicted its success. Now in *Capital* he thought he had demonstrated its inevitability, the result of the self-destructive character of capitalism, doomed to perish by its own inherent contradictions: "The centralization of the means of production and the socialization of labor reach a point where they prove incompatible with their capitalist husk. This bursts asunder. The knell of capitalist private property sounds. The expropriators are expropriated."

Marx thought that his conclusion was the verdict of social and economic science. More evident to us is the face and voice of the angry Hebrew prophet, denouncing the worship of the golden calf and the human sacrifices to a mechanical Moloch and trumpeting the wrath to come in the careless ears of the unrighteous. Capital is a "fetish," a false god. Marx's intellectual career comes full circle; the face of the economic theorist melts into that of the young idealist philosopher, to whom the ultimate evil is the subjection of mind and spirit to the domination of brute *things*.

J. W. Burrow, a young professor at the University of East Anglia in Norwich, England, is the author of Evolution and Society: A Study of Victorian Social Theory. *He wrote the article on Charles Darwin for the Autumn, 1966,* HORIZON.

CONSTANT AND THE KING OF SIAM

Here is the tale of an exceptional man brought low (again, alas) by the awesome forces of the commonplace

In 1648 or thereabouts the great lottery of fate tossed a winning number to the Greek island of Cephalonia. It fell in the cradle of Konstantine Gerakis, a poor tavern-keeper's son. "Gerakis" means "Falcon"; the surname fitted the recipient better than do most. Later he found it convenient to translate the name into Western form; and thus history remembers him, though with an effort, as Constant Phaulkon.

When he was about ten, he shipped as cabin boy aboard an English trading vessel. A likely lad, he learned seamanship and fluent English and the arithmetic of profit and loss. He joined the Church of England, no doubt more from policy than conviction. When about twenty-two, he went out to the East as cabin boy on an East Indiaman and attracted the favorable notice of the supercargo (or captain?), George White. He and White deserted the East India Company and traded independently, as "interlopers," from the Persian Gulf to Indonesia. Phaulkon, who had already picked up Portuguese and Malay on his travels, added Siamese to his linguistic stock and made many valuable business contacts.

He now bought a half-interest in the sloop *Mary*, and acting as master, set off on a trading trip to Sumatra. But he wrecked the *Mary* somewhere on the way. He met on the shore the Siamese ambassador to Persia, likewise shipwrecked, whom he brought safely back to Siam in a small boat, and was rewarded by introductions and recommendations to the barcalon and other high officials.

The story has a rather fabulous sound, but the *Mary* was certainly wrecked, and Phaulkon certainly appears soon after as the controller of commerce for the kingdom of Siam.

He had recognized and seized that opportunity of which every ambitious man dreams. The door to power briefly opened before him, and he boldly entered.

The circumstances were propitious. The king of Siam, Narai, an intelligent and genial monarch, held the monopoly on his country's foreign trade. Operations were in the hands of Mohammedan Indonesians working

Constant Phaulkon, kneeling, exhorts a French ambassador to raise the bowl containing a letter from Louis XIV to within reach of Narai, the king of Siam.

with the Dutch merchant fleet. Their graft was monumental and was undisturbed by the Siamese ministers, sunk in pride and sloth. When Phaulkon was appointed Chief Merchant, he arrested and tortured the leading Indonesians and suppressed all speculations except, of course, his own. The king, in gratitude, made him a high-class mandarin and conferred on him a hat hung with bells. The king proposed further to install him as his barcalon. But Phaulkon refused, recognizing the hostility that would

ensue and preferring the reality of power to its semblance.

The king was an absolute ruler, whose holiness set him above all ordinary humanity. He dwelt hidden in his palace, only rarely showing his face even to his ministers. But he was bored by his solitary eminence. He made Phaulkon his confidant and companion and could not be parted from him for a day.

Phaulkon repaid the king's favor with genuine devotion. He was a man of great personal charm, lusty and gusty, with an insinuating manner. He held men spellbound with his fiery eyes, wherein lurked something dark and mysterious, and he had a remarkable range of knowledge.

In 1682 he was reconverted to Catholicism, his childhood faith. He proved a zealous Christian, rising daily at five to spend an hour in pious meditation before beginning the day's business. Twice a week he fed the poor, and on Holy Thursdays he washed the feet of twelve beggars and served them dinner, on his knees, to general bewilderment.

Religion was not allowed to interfere with business—quite the reverse, in fact. Siam's foreign trade was restricted by the jealous power of the Dutch East India Company. Phaulkon proposed to combat it by calling in the French. He filled the king's mind with tales of Louis XIV's might and magnificence, and he sent gift-laden ambassadors to the Sun King. They bore letters appealing to Louis's cupidity by promising great returns in trade, and to his piety by hinting that King Narai was ripe for conversion to Catholic Christianity.

King Louis, readily persuaded, sent out an expedition in the spring of 1685 under the command of an ambassador, the Chevalier de Chaumont. He

By MORRIS BISHOP

added a number of ecclesiastics, including six learned Jesuits.

After a seven-month voyage, the envoys disembarked in Siam. They were transported up the river Menam in the king's splendid galleys, and in the capital, Ayuthia, were magnificently welcomed by Phaulkon. The letter from Louis to the king of Siam, on its golden salver, was convoyed separately, in a glittering gilded barge.

Here a knotty problem of etiquette presented itself. Ambassador Chaumont wished to hand Louis's letter directly to the king. Phaulkon protested that the ambassador must lie prostrate in the king's presence. After several messages to and fro, permission was granted to the ambassador to stand at the solemn moment. Therefore, at the palace door, the Abbé de Choisy took the letter and placed it on a golden bowl supported by a three-and-a-half-foot staff. Trumpets and drums sounded; Chaumont, Choisy, and Phaulkon marched to the audience chamber between two rows of a thousand soldiers sitting on their heels. The room was filled with prostrate mandarins, but the envoys saw no king until he showed himself enthroned, peering out through a small window some six feet above the ground. The mandarins clasped their hands behind their heads and knocked their foreheads resoundingly on the floor. Phaulkon removed his slippers and crawled on all fours toward the window. Chaumont doffed his hat and made three obeisances in the French style. He then read a very ill-timed address summoning Narai to join the Roman Catholic Church. Fortunately only the French understood it.

Now came the holy moment of the presentation of Louis's letter. Chaumont took the golden bowl in his hand. To reach Narai he would have to hold the staff at its base and raise the bowl high. This action, he felt, was beneath the dignity of France; he would bend his elbow, not raise his arm from the shoulder. Phaulkon, crouching on the floor, cried in agony:

"Higher! Higher!" But the king, smiling at barbarian punctilio, graciously leaned down from his window, took the letter, and placed it on his head. A great sigh of relief filled the chamber.

Chaumont and the other French envoys had several further audiences with the king. Chaumont, a recent and zealous convert from Protestantism, dwelt forever on the proofs of Catholicism. The king was bored; he had expected business deals and an alliance against the Dutch. He said, with Buddhist tolerance, that all religions are true and all are imposed by God to meet the needs of diverse nations.

However, the visitors were more than royally entertained. They inspected the famous white elephant, fed only from gold vessels and attended by four mandarins, who fanned him and shaded his eyes with parasols. Phaulkon took them on hunts, guiding his own elephant, a sports model, at a spirited trot. He treated them to magnificent festivities that included fireworks, jugglers, and tumblers, and a very long and tiresome Chinese opera.

The diplomatic mission was counted a success by both parties. Two years later Louis XIV sent out a military-religious mission with fourteen Jesuits, 636 officers and soldiers, and magnificent presents and kindly letters to the king and to Phaulkon.

Meanwhile, however, Phaulkon's standing deteriorated. He weathered a rebellion prompted by the Indonesians and Malays, but his enemies were gaining strength. And the king was ill from a gathering dropsy.

Now in 1688, a Siamese strong man, P'ra P'et Rāchā, Keeper of the Royal Elephants, mounted a full-scale rebellion. Phaulkon scorned the advice of the French that he abdicate his post and flee to France. The French commander refused to commit his troops. P'ra P'et Rāchā invaded the royal palace and seized Phaulkon and the dying king. The king's two younger brothers were respectfully inserted into sacks of scarlet velvet and

pounded to death with sandalwood clubs, "which is in Siam a torture reserved for persons of the highest consideration." The heir to the throne, Narai's adopted son, was beheaded. Phaulkon was led to the execution place in the forest. He knelt, prayed, and protested his innocence of imputed crimes. He was then beheaded by a backhand saber-blow, according to Siamese ritual.

Shortly afterward the king died and was succeeded by P'ra P'et Rāchā. The French sailed away. An antiforeign and anti-Christian spirit possessed the country, and Siam remained off limits to Western traders for a century and a half.

And what of the great Phaulkon, who died at forty, after rising from cabin boy to effective ruler of a kingdom? Does he inform us at all of the human lot? His contemporaries applaud his intelligence, his quick wit, his decision, his courage, his impatience with verbiage and circumlocution, his "magnificence," or lavishness, his charm, and his apparently genuine piety. Turning the coin, they reprove his pride, cruelty, violence of temper, greed for honors, if not money, and his vanity and unappeasable ambition. But a man is more than a sum of qualities; he is an indivisible entity. One who knew him speaks of his "indescribable air of authority."

This, I think, is the clue. The dominant man, the great man, in government, business, all human relations, possesses the indescribable air of authority. This comes from within; it cannot be learned or taught. It expresses a quality of spirit beyond our definition. He who owns it is driven to mastery despite himself, and in the end he is likely to be undone by fate's backhand saber-blow, representing the victory of the commonplace over the exceptional. This is a favorite theme of ancient Greek tragedy; and Phaulkon's story is a modern Greek tragedy.

This is the third in a series of biographical escapades by Morris Bishop.

THE COMPLEAT AMERICAN PRAGMATIST

Race crisis? Urban decay? Revolution?
Consider not the problems, but one of the men who works
to solve them: Daniel Patrick Moynihan

One way or another, nearly everyone has heard of Daniel Patrick Moynihan. Director of the Harvard-M.I.T. Joint Center for Urban Studies, he runs the most prestigious of the "think tanks" concerned with the problems of that environment in which most of us make our livings and try to make a life—the American city. He is co-author of *Beyond the Melting Pot*, a well-known and well-regarded volume describing how various immigrant groups got to New York City and how they have made out there. He was the youngest sub-cabinet officer in the New Frontier, eventually becoming Assistant Secretary of Labor, and he lingered in Washington long enough to write one of the most controversial public documents of the Johnson administration. It was the now famous "Moynihan Report," which advanced the thesis that much of the social disorganization of the slums stems from the disintegration of traditional family patterns among Negroes.

All of these activities—not to mention Moynihan's apparently congenital love of controversy and publicity —make him ever available as article writer, speechmaker, television personality, seminar participant, and interviewee for itinerant journalists. They have also placed him in some danger of becoming a certifiable celebrity, and his public image keeps intruding on any critical attempt to discuss his ideas. The problem is deepened by Moynihan's preference for scattering ideas at random and his disinclination to fit them together in a coherent, more easily approachable system. It is further complicated by the fact that his field is new, wide-ranging, and an object of some suspicion among intellectuals. Indeed, there is as yet no decent word to describe Moynihan's profession. No sensible man can label himself by such a mouthful as "student of urban affairs"—or by the vulgar made-word "urbanologist," which is currently in vogue. He must draw on many disciplines—political science, economics, sociology, psychology, history, the law, even old-fashioned city planning, which itself is an interdisciplinary stew—without being able to invoke the traditions and authority of any of them.

Moynihan has been variously and unsatisfactorily termed a neoconservative, a pragmatic liberal, and a Victorian missionary. The best neutral description of him was supplied by a popular magazine that called him "Idea Broker in the Race Crisis," but even that slightly misses the mark. He is, more simply, an American of that classic type so often described by students of the national character from De Tocqueville on. Which is to say that he has an abiding faith in the long-term viability of our system and is impatient with ideologically based attempts to improve it, especially those that toy with revolutionary doctrines. He is a rational man whose ultimate test of an idea is a very American one: he cares little about its correctness in terms of some abstract sociopolitical theory and very much about whether it will work as its advocates predict— actually providing more jobs, more housing, better education, or what have you.

Over and over again Moynihan insists on two points: that the American system works better than anything anyone else has tried or even imagined —and that it can be made to work still more effectively. With most of the intellectual establishment thrilling to the news that the Negro revolution and the war in Vietnam have contrived, in journalist Andrew Kopkind's phrase, to "murder liberalism in its official robes," and titillating itself with visions of an imminent apocalypse, Daniel Patrick Moynihan remains firmly, even fervently, convinced that the condition of man has improved. "Things are better," he said in his 1967 Phi Beta Kappa address at Harvard, "and where they are best is in the liberal industrial democracies of the North Atlantic world. I hold these regimes to be the best accommodation to the human condition yet devised, and will demand to know of those who reject it, just what they have in mind as a replacement."

This does not mean, however, that he rejects the revitalizing effect revolutionary ideas and movements have demonstrably had on these societies. He notes that historically it has been

By RICHARD SCHICKEL

possible to incorporate the most serviceable revolutionary ideas into our culture without tearing it down. Moynihan regards the revolutionary process itself as a remarkably inefficient way of restructuring society, destroying as it does so many useful people and institutions. Moreover, no one who has been raised a Catholic is likely to regard the basic belief of the revolutionary sensibility—that an earthly paradise is possible—as much more than a fantasy that makes no allowance for the immutable disruptiveness of original sin.

Committed to rationalism and to the liberal democratic system, Moynihan is nevertheless committed to very little else about our present social structure. Indeed, he believes that if the basic system is to survive its current crisis, it must completely re-evaluate the programs and policies by which it has attempted—and manifestly failed—to realize the goal of a socially and economically fluid society for everyone. Liberals no less than conservatives—and probably more so—are emotionally and philosophically fixated upon a set of assumptions about Negroes, the city, and the poor that are, he says, quite simply wrong. The only time a note of despair creeps into Moynihan's work is when he contemplates the possibility that somehow we may fail to meet our present crisis with the same kind of ingenuity that we have mustered in similarly dark moments in the past.

In the past decade there has been no shortage of presidential commissions investigating the most serious of our social problems or of investigative interest on the part of government agencies. The trouble is that many of the most interesting policy suggestions from both sources have been either untested or unfairly tried as a result of legislative parsimony, while other, less worthy, ideas have been foisted on us, not because they were the best solution to a problem, but because they best fitted certain unquestioned as-

sumptions. There is no better example of this than our attempts to deal with the problems of poverty. Moynihan has written that in "trying to be kind, trying to be helpful, we somehow have got in the habit of denying the reality of the life circumstances of the lower class which has curiously paralyzed our ability to do anything to change these realities." The most notorious examples of this habit were the initial refusals of the White House to accept the reports of the Crime and Riot commissions when they were delivered and its attempt to suppress "The People Left Behind," the report of the presidential commission on rural poverty.

This sort of thing appalls Moynihan. He has a respect for facts that borders on awe, and he finds it difficult to accept the notion that people will carelessly miss or willfully ignore the painfully acquired information on which effective social theory and planning must be based.

There are, he observes, several reasons for their ambivalence about research. Research may, for instance, demonstrate that a well-publicized, generally favored program is not achieving the effects it is supposed to achieve, which can be very embarrassing to its public champions. Unfortunately, social science data are never neutral. "Most social arrangements rest on assumptions about the 'facts' of a given situation. To challenge such facts is also to challenge those social arrangements," Moynihan told a Senate hearing in the winter of 1966, and he quoted social scientist Walter B. Miller, who has suggested that there may be "a direct incompatibility between careful evaluative research and the political process."

Characteristically, Moynihan refuses to give up on this point. As he observed in the same hearings, evaluation research is a comparatively new tool for social change, and so far it has inevitably been controlled by the executive rather than the legislative branches at all levels of government.

This puts the latter at a considerable disadvantage when debating alternatives, leads to the suppression of inconvenient information by the executive agencies, and puts pressure on the independent bodies that do the research under contract to come up with positive findings about existing programs.

What is needed, Moynihan told the senators, is a system of checking and balancing this monopoly; he proposed that Congress set up an "Office of Legislative Evaluation" to test and measure the effectiveness of "all the social and economic programs enacted by it and paid for out of public monies." In the absence of any such official evaluative and reportorial agency, Moynihan has undertaken to do a good deal of its work himself. As we shall see, most of the controversy that has surrounded him has been generated not because he advanced some wild new scheme for social change but because he broke the conspiracy of silence surrounding some indigestible bit of knowledge.

Moynihan's guiding faiths—in the basic viability of American democracy and in the ability of social science research to improve its performance—are based on intense personal experience. He is convinced that America can be a land of opportunity for everyone, because it was for him. Born in 1927 in Tulsa, Oklahoma, he moved to New York and grew up poor in such insalubrious climates as Hell's Kitchen and Harlem, where he peddled newspapers and ran a shoeshine stand. He took entrance exams for the City College of New York with a stevedore's hook hanging from his pocket, moved on with the aid of the Navy's wartime V-12 program and scholarships to Middlebury, Tufts, and the London School of Economics, and ultimately won his Ph.D. from the Fletcher School of Law and Diplomacy at Tufts. In the process he learned that for an ambitious, intellectually prepared man the American Dream can still be a reality. This knowledge is implicit in everything Moynihan writes and says, and it is the quality that definitively sets his work apart from the more hysterical—and currently more fashionable—theorists of our present crisis. It also accounts, no doubt, for the highly personal quality of some of the attacks on him.

His faith in the power of research stems from an experience that occurred during his first job in government. In 1953 he went to work as an assistant to W. Averell Harriman and later served under him when Harriman became governor of New York. Assigned to a committee investigating the traffic safety problem, Moynihan was startled by the request of a scientist representing the state public health service for the research report on which the scientist automatically assumed the group's discussion would be based. There was none.

Everyone had simply thought that traffic safety was merely a matter of better laws and better law enforcement, driver education, and, perhaps, an intensified public relations campaign for safety. None of these approaches was exactly untried and none was exactly successful, as the ever-rising accident rate indicated. The committee decided to do a little basic research before drafting its proposals, and its subsequent report virtually reinvented the subject of traffic safety. It decided that in attacking the psychology of the individual driver—as all the accepted techniques were doing—it was attacking the problem in the least effective way. The committee proceeded to examine road safety as a public health problem rather than as a legal or moral one. Was there not too much emphasis on fixing blame and meting out punishment to violators of traffic laws? Might it not be easier to convince the handful of people in Detroit who design cars to build them so that accidents would be less frequently fatal, instead of trying to change the behavioral patterns of millions of drivers?

The road to Ralph Nader was now open, and it is no accident that it was Moynihan who brought him to Washington and to the position from which he launched his crusade for safer cars. Nor is it coincidence that it is in the field of highway safety that Moynihan has made his most original scholarly (as opposed to journalistic and educational) contributions. Recently he has written a great deal about the need for a new form of automobile insurance. Not surprisingly, he advocates one that would dispense with the necessity of finding who is to blame for an accident, which might, in turn, free our overcrowded courts from their demeaning preoccupation with automobile claims cases.

Moynihan says there is "a lot of analogy" between the problem of automobile safety and the admittedly far more complex ones posed by the modern American city. As with the car, we lack adequate data on the city and have misread what we do possess. As a result we have not yet separated those things that government can effectively manage from those it cannot.

He maintains, quoting from James Q. Wilson, his predecessor as head of the Joint Center, that "for the present, the urban Negro is, in a fundamental sense, *the* urban problem." At the same time he is quick to point out "that we make fewer and fewer distinctions between those issues which are correctly defined as having to do with race, and those much more accurately, and usefully defined as matters of social class." As he wrote in *Commentary* last May in a brief for the presidential candidacy of Robert F. Kennedy: "There is precious little government seems able to do about racial feeling, whereas there is a great deal that can be done about class problems. . . . This is not to deny that the problem of racism is agonizingly real in the United States, and that it is the source of the lower-class status of so many urban Negroes. But it is to assert that when the issue at hand is a recognizable problem of lower-class behavior—crime, violence, welfare dependency, low educational achievement, certain kinds of unemployment, or whatever—behavior as much to be found within white groups of the same income and class level, not much good and very likely some harm is done by turning directly to the subject of white guilt. Once again attention is diverted from the Negro community, where the problem and the need are both located . . ."

This position is easier taken than advanced, as Moynihan discovered a few years ago when he wrote the "Moynihan Report." He came to the subject in a typical fashion. One day, when he was still in the labor department, he happened to notice a three-inch story in the Washington *Post* reporting that 50 per cent of the young men called for the draft failed either the mental or physical exam. Who, exactly, were the rejected 50 per cent? Burrowing through his beloved statistics, he isolated the factor that seemed to lie behind the majority of the selective service rejections: family background and, more specifically, the Negro family. Fewer than 50 per cent of all Negroes reach the age of eighteen having lived their lives with both parents; 21 per cent of all Negro families are fatherless; somewhere between 25 and 40 per cent of all Negro children are illegitimate. "The evidence—not final, but powerfully persuasive—is that the Negro family in the urban ghettos is crumbling. For vast numbers, the fabric of conventional social relationships has all but disintegrated."

Circulating privately in government circles, the report was at first greeted with praise—at last someone had said what many people suspected but few had dared to admit openly. Passages were incorporated by President Johnson into his Howard University speech on the Negro problem. Then a reaction set in. Basing their charges on isolated quotations from the report that were leaked to the press, many Negro leaders and white liberals accused Moynihan of racism, or at least of aiding and comforting segregationists.

Nothing could have been further from his intention. His report consistently treated Negroes as a *class*, not as a race, and called for government programs to assist them in overcoming problems imposed upon them by a century of class deprivation rather than racial discrimination. He has come to believe that our traditional welfare programs do not attack in a fundamental way the issue of class, but instead meddle around the edges of the issue in an ineffective and often alienating fashion. He prefers a direct, across-the-board approach: "Beef up the family income and everything else will follow in its train," he has said.

He has lately extended criticism of the kind he leveled at our conventional welfare wisdom to our ideas about educating what he calls "the urban underclass." For years the assumption has been that slum children lag behind those of the middle class in educational achievement because of the lower quality of their schools, their teachers, and their curriculums. Moynihan points to a report principally written by James S. Coleman and titled *Equality of Educational Opportunity*. It challenged this assumption on the basis of the most impressive statistical survey ever made on the issue, and its 738 pages were seen, quite correctly, by the bureaucrats of the Department of Health, Education, and Welfare as dynamite. In July of 1966 they put out a fifty-two-page summary of its findings that was deliberately misleading, released it over a holiday weekend when no one pays attention to the newspapers, and subsequently allowed the report to go out of print.

Coleman indicated that the quality of education offered in slum schools was not significantly different from that offered in middle-class public schools and that the differences that did exist had little discernible effect on the achievements of students. Even such treasured bits of conventional wisdom as the notion that a low teacher-pupil ratio (i.e., small classes) automatically means better education

did not stand up under examination. Coleman's findings echoed Moynihan's: more than anyone else, Negro children suffer from the instability of their family backgrounds. Educationally they do not get the support from their families and from their fellow students that white middle-class children do. Their performance improves when they are desegregated by bussing or by some other means, although this has a highly undesirable side effect: their white classmates do less well in this situation than they do in an all-white school. What the Coleman report says is that none of the most popular remedies for the lag in Negro education will work, and that is a very hard truth to swallow.

Again, for the long haul Moynihan advocates more money for the families. In effect he is saying that educational tinkering is no more useful than welfare tinkering and that what is needed is a massive effort to turn the lower class into a working class. He is not, however, convinced that either the federal government or the liberal establishment (at least as it is presently constituted) can do the job. "The federal government is good at collecting revenues, and rather bad at disbursing services," he says. Moreover, he thinks that in the nuclear age the national government will always give priority to foreign affairs and that "a system has to be developed, therefore, under which domestic programs go forward regardless of what international crisis is preoccupying Washington at the moment. This in effect means decentralizing the initiative and the resources for such programs." It also means that state and municipal government, if it is "to assume an effective role as an innovative and creative agent . . . must begin to receive a share of federal revenues on a permanent, ongoing basis." Private business, too, must be involved in a systematic, purposeful manner in domestic programs: "What aero-space corporations have done for getting us

to the moon, urban housing corporations can do for the slums."

All of this is, of course, anathema to the liberal establishment, most of whose ideas were formed in the Roosevelt era. Moynihan is suspected of collaborating with the conservatives, a charge that he cheerfully refuses to deny, citing conservative economist Milton Friedman's plan for a negative income tax and Representative Melvin Laird's call for direct federal aid to states and cities as "two of the most interesting program proposals in years." He chastises liberals for paying too much attention to the sources of such ideas and not enough to their intrinsic merits.

Criticism of this kind earns plenty of criticism in return. In the academic community both Moynihan and many of his colleagues are suspected of being dabblers, men whose scholarly credentials are not quite in order.

Lee Rainwater and Willam L. Yancey, who edited *The Moynihan Report and the Politics of Controversy*, were forced to concede that the report "is not basically a research report or a technical document; it is a polemic which makes use of social science techniques and findings to convince others." They feel that it must be evaluated as an example of higher journalism, a document that "selects some crucial issues and presents them in such a way as not to belie a fuller and more balanced intellectual discussion." They think—as I do—that the report meets the best standards of this kind of writing, and so, one must add, does most of Moynihan's work. But, Rainwater and Yancey add, "we recognize that some . . . social scientists would disagree."

They certainly do. David M. Schneider, an anthropologist at the University of Chicago, has written—somewhat cloudily—that the report was "bad politics because it generated controversy instead of being the call to arms that was intended." Also, he says, "it was bad social science," perhaps suitable to a less sophisticated age, but today reading "too much like a white, urban, middle-class, Protestant of almost Victorian vintage vigorously reaffirming his middle-class values and deploring the degeneracy of the Lower Orders, bound to undertake some uplifting missionary activity among them for their own good."

This view would find support on all levels of the Negro community. Journalist Garry Wills, in his excellent study "The Second Civil War," tells of an encounter with two Negro policemen who deplored the matriarchy for the way it has set the tone of ghetto life; they noted that militant Negro youth is as much in revolt against it as it is against white society. At the same time they heaped scorn on Moynihan for making essentially the same arguments: "What that cat knows about us colored boys I could put in my eyeball." Black militants, naturally, have gone even farther. If the quality of their ghetto civilization is to be questioned, Rap Brown has said, then it is time "to talk about the civilization of Lyndon Johnson, to talk about the civilization of James O. Eastland, to talk about the civilization of Patrick Moynihan"—which is about as nonsensical a bit of associative guilt as one can imagine.

But, as Moynihan continually insists, if the Black militants bothered to read what he has written, they would see that his diagnosis of their ills is point-for-point the same as theirs and that his call for an end to the old, meddling social-work tradition and for the establishment of a simple, unpatronizing boost in incomes and social opportunities is quite similar to theirs.

But such attacks are not confined to the obviously ill-informed members of "the urban underclass," which, he says, has been driven "half-crazy" by the denial of fundamental human rights and economic opportunities. Perhaps more galling to him is the attitude of the New Left, described by Moynihan as "radical, nihilist youth . . . determined to use [the un-derclass] as an instrument of a violent apocalyptic confrontation with a white society they have determined to be irredeemably militaristic and racist." Like many who came of age in the 1940's and 1950's, he has an instinctive distrust of leftist ideologies (though not necessarily of the left's fundamental goals). The anticommunism that marked that era taught certain lessons in the need for tough-mindedness that may well have to be learned anew by this generation.

In short, Moynihan has lately found himself more and more in a position where he has almost no one to talk to. In the spring of 1968 it obviously seemed to him that Robert Kennedy was the last person with whom he could make common cause, the last American politician who had the ability to turn a cadre drawn from all points of the political compass into a new liberal coalition that could replace the battered one that Roosevelt shaped so long ago.

Moynihan likes to tell a story that illustrates just how essential the ability to weld such a coalition is in a modern democracy. A British expert in guerrilla warfare was once asked why American efforts to teach the rudiments of orderly self-government in underdeveloped countries always seemed to fail. "Elemental," he replied. "You teach them all your techniques, give them all the machinery and manuals of operation and standards of performance, and the more you do it the more they become convinced and bitterly resentful of the fact, as they see it, that you are deliberately withholding from them the one all-important secret that you have and they do not, and that is the knowledge of how to trust one another."

Trust—between individuals, between groups, between government and its citizens. Moynihan is convinced that it is historically the most significant creation of the American mind and spirit. And this belief leads him to the corollary conviction that the most basic issue facing us today "is to retain that large and still preponderant trust that remains, and to regain that which has been lost."

In this mad political season it is an open question whether that sense of mutual trust is, in fact, "large and still preponderant." It is entirely possible that the events of recent years have severely crippled it and that Moynihan's statement of its condition is more an act of desperate faith than a completely accurate description of reality. If so, then it is hard to imagine just where he—or anyone else who shares his bias toward rational, pragmatic, technically oriented, locally based, one-step-at-a-time political action—will go. Closely related is a partly emotional, partly intellectual prejudice against mass political activity that may inevitably lead Moynihan and people like him toward the right. Certainly the present hysteria on the left, with its implicit anarchy, can only accelerate that drift. All of us who are old-fashioned liberals feel the pull as we try to preserve a decent respect for the singularity of the individual and his right to dissent from the ignorantly overpoliticalized opinions of the mob, which, particularly on the campuses, has been trampling out a brutally scornful vintage of late.

Whether Moynihan or any other member of the elite he describes as "trained to be skeptical, enquiring, and demanding of a great deal of information before they give assent to any individual or policy" can in the near future re-establish a trusting relationship with all the groups that are in a state of near rebellion is, perhaps, the most serious question now confronting the nation. If they cannot, then Moynihan's future—and that of most liberal establishmentarians—is likely to be that of a Jeremiah. It is very hard to keep your head when all about you are losing theirs.

Richard Schickel is a free-lance writer and the regular movie reviewer for Life *magazine. His most recent book is a biography:* The Disney Version.

Somewhere Else with Allen and Gregory

It all started in Paris in the spring of 1958,
when the young British poet Dom Moraes invited Allen Ginsberg
and Gregory Corso to visit Oxford. They did

On our first morning in Paris, sitting in the Deux Magots with my friend K., I suddenly saw two unkempt and unshaven young men bounding toward us and recognized one of them as Allen Ginsberg, the beat poet, whom I had met briefly in London a few weeks before. Ginsberg's face had not at that time assumed the considerable quantity of foliage that was later to enshroud it. It was a sad, intelligent face, with large eyes that stared through thick spectacles. His companion was Gregory Corso, the other leading beat poet, a stocky yet faunlike young man with a wild look and an incessant flow of conversation. They sat down with us, and Corso asked K., "Would you like to ball with me, baby?" There was no surer way to K.'s heart. She declined with a small, secretive, pleased smile and at once exerted herself to be charming. Ginsberg and Corso seemed oblivious to these efforts: Ginsberg fixed me with a sad stare and demanded to know my views on God, man, and poetry. When I was slow to answer, he told me his, in a rapid and hypnotized voice, at great length, and then fell into a deep silence, head bent and hands locked between his knees. Corso meanwhile described his experience of communicating with God as he watched a corpse being fished out of the Seine. Eventually they left, inviting us to breakfast next day in their hotel on rue Git-le-Coeur.

We went. Ginsberg and Corso lived in an attic of the hotel, which they shared with William Burroughs, the author of *The Naked Lunch*. The attic held three pallet beds and a quantity of beat literature stored away in suitcases that contained nothing else. Ginsberg and Corso scattered this literature over one of the beds and advised me to read it, while Burroughs, a tall, angular man with a gray face, rolled up his trousers and showed K. the network of needle marks that covered his legs. When a pigeon moaned at the window, he hastily rolled his trousers down and said in a quiet flat voice, "Birds. I hate birds."

There was no sign of breakfast, but eventually Corso produced a sack from under the bed, fished some marijuana out, and rolled us all cigarettes. Then the two poets dragged us off to meet the painter Larry Rivers. Rivers had a young American woman with him, and they leapt at her, suggesting that we all strip and make love on the pavement. "Like William Blake and the angels, man," cried Corso. The girl became upset and burst into tears, and the poets were much concerned, petting her with repentant hands and offering her poems and candy that Corso pulled from his pockets.

After that we spent a lot of time with Ginsberg and Corso. I came to like them both very much. Corso had immense charm, the charm of a wicked schoolboy, which he used very consciously. Ginsberg was very serious and given to long silences; though some of his statements seemed absurd, they were absurd in a consistent, rather beautiful way. He told me, for instance, that in his poem *Howl* he had invented a new kind of prosody, undreamed of before, and that he had had a vision of William Blake in his apartment in Harlem. I inquired what Blake had worn to the interview. "Oh, like a toga, man," Ginsberg said, "the kind of clothes all the people wore in those days." He also told me of his first encounter with Corso. "Gregory was just out of prison," said Ginsberg reverently, "and one day I went into this bar in Greenwich Village, and he was sitting at a table. He was beating it with his fist, like, and shouting that he was a great poet. So of course I knew at once he was a great poet."

And they were both poets; neither could have been anything else. Their methods were far from mine: they believed in verbal extravagance and visions. I didn't, but I respected their beliefs. Also I admired some of their work. I invited them to visit Oxford in the summer and to read their poetry there.

As summer put flowers back in the college quadrangles, Ginsberg and Corso announced their impending arrival. I went up to London to collect them, and on our arrival at Oxford, a reception committee consisting of Peter Levi, Quentin Stevenson, and Del Kolve met us. Our tour around Oxford was crowded with difficulties. I took Gregory to look at Shelley lying obscene in white marble at University College. He inquired whether he was allowed to kiss the statue's foot. I said probably not. He then demanded to know where Shelley's rooms were. I had not the faintest idea but indicated the nearest door. I hadn't dreamed that he would want to enter, but he did; he flung open the door and crawled over the carpet, kissing it reverently, inch by inch, while its occupant, who prior to his arrival had been making tea, stared at him in dumbfounded silence.

Later the visitors demanded to see W. H. Auden. Auden had specifically forbidden me to bring any beat poet anywhere near him, but they found out where he lived from someone else, and since I could not prevent the visit, I went along. Auden, though sur-

By DOM MORAES

Corso and Ginsberg, 1958

prised, was very tolerant. He either ignored Allen's remarks on prosody or received them with noncommital grunts. He then offered to show the beats around Christ Church Cathedral, and did so. At the end both Allen and Gregory turned to him with tears in their eyes. This, they said, was the high point of their visit to Oxford: they could never forget how a great poet had shown them around a cathedral. They knelt and attempted to kiss the hem of Auden's garments—the cuffs of his trousers, to be exact. Auden hastily stepped out of reach, gruffly said his good-byes, and departed. Allen and Gregory got up and dusted their knees. "That was a drag," said Gregory. "Man, we went right around this church with a guidebook yesterday." This curious mixture of innocence combined with a sharp eye for the main chance was attractive. Somehow everybody took to the visitors.

We took the poets punting; they smoked marijuana as we eddied over green, scumbled water in which trees trailed their arms. As we passed under Magdalene Bridge amidst liquid shadows, the boom of a bell came to us through the yellow stone overhead. Gregory said in a childish, wistful way, "I wish I'd been to school here."

They stayed for several days. During their visit Edith Sitwell arrived in Oxford to read at the town hall. Quentin took Allen and Gregory and me to the rehearsal. A large John Piper screen had been set up on the platform, and to it, presently, came Dame Edith, in a long sibilant dress on which dark, heavy necklaces faintly swung and clashed. She looked frail but very queenly, and she offered us her hand like a holy relic. Allen, however, was unimpressed. He told her that he was editing an anthology of verse illustrated with photographs of the poets in the nude and asked her if she would like to contribute. Fortunately Dame Edith took this well and declined in the most courteous way. She also rejected an offer of marijuana from Gregory because, she said, it made her feel ill. I thought she had the best manners of anyone I had ever met.

Later, however, when in her customary fashion she had retired behind the Piper screen and was moaning effectively behind it, things changed. The screen was not properly attached; it was swaying about, and she demanded to know why this was so. She demanded it once only, but the tone of her voice set people into manic activity. It was no use. Eventually several bystanders, including Allen and Gregory, were commanded to hold the screen steady at each end. Dame Edith resumed; but barely a minute had passed when unexpectedly the screen tilted forward and fell with a resounding crash, hurling its supporters in all directions. The only ones undamaged were Allen and Gregory, who stood back with curious little smiles as Dame Edith rose on the now naked stage and demanded in outraged tones: "What is the matter, pray?" Her voice brought all the bruised and dolorous bodies lying around her to their feet, and forgetful of their own sorrows, they rushed to reassure the great poet. Later Quentin said thoughtfully to me, "Someone *pushed* that screen, you know."

Things became more frantic toward the end of the visit. Even then, in 1958, they had numerous English supporters and imitators, and a reading that took place at New College

Ginsberg and Corso, 1968

was a disaster largely because it was invaded by numbers of them. The hosts, the college poetry society, were understandably exasperated. One hairy young man with large, bare, smelly feet ambled in and stretched himself out on a sofa. There he rolled a marijuana cigarette. The ceiling of the room was low, and to the astonishment of everyone else present he placed a match between his toes, struck it on the ceiling with a careless sweep of the foot, and lit his cigarette.

Quite apart from the uninvited hordes, the reading itself was not a success. I had forgotten to advise Allen and Gregory that New College was a stronghold of the Campaign for Nuclear Disarmament. When Gregory began to read a poem about the aesthetic pleasures of a nuclear explosion, his hosts were outraged. There was a great deal of heckling, and finally the New College poetry society, led by Stephen Hugh-Jones, the editor of *Isis*, took off their shoes and threw them at the poets. Allen and Gregory packed up their poems and left. They were tight-lipped and silent, with hurt eyes, like children who have been chastised for the first time. Peter Levi and I, indulgent nannies, nursed them out of their hurt, and the night, their last in Oxford, ended in riotous laughter.

I never saw Ginsberg again, but Gregory and I met frequently over the years, in London and Paris. Last time I saw him he was lying on a bed in a large empty room in the Plaza, saying bitterly, "Allen's off on this holy kick, and I'm finished with the beat stuff. When I tell people I'm not a beat, I'm a poet, they don't believe me. They don't believe I've grown up." He shook his head uncomprehendingly and turned away.

Dom Moraes is a thirty-year-old poet, a winner of the Hawthornden Prize, born in India and now living in England. This article will form part of his memoirs, which are soon to be published by the Macmillan Company.

THE TALE
OF THE
PURLOINED SAINT

In medieval Christendom every hamlet had to have its saintly relics. Lacking any, the holy
fathers of Conques set about acquiring some and found that crime, occasionally, does pay

Yes, saintforsaken was the word for it. A girdle of angry cliff faces, a murmur of mountain waters, a shiver of naked poplars by the arched Roman bridge, and there suddenly it was, half-hidden by the rocky ledge guarding the entrance to the secluded valley: the little town of Conques, a cluster of gabled roofs and timbered walls watched over on the left by a tiny helmeted castle and in the center by the rainwashed bulk of its basilica, as squat and stoop-shouldered as a medieval man-at-arms. A pale winter sun cast a faint clambering shadow across the tufts of brownish grass as I trudged up the *chemin de Charlemagne*, trying not to slide back down its mossy flagstones. I doubt that the great Frankish emperor ever got near this remote mountain glen, but it was up this steep and slippery slope that for centuries the pilgrims struggled with their mules, though few of them can have been so foolhardy as to undertake the trek in midwinter.

Farther up, by the basilica, I found the Auberge de Sainte-Foy resolutely shut, its ornate ironwork sign deceptively promising hearthside warmth and Yuletide cheer. But a few steps down—for half the streets of Conques are steps—was a weather-beaten hostelry dimly advertising itself as the "Hôtel Boudou." I sat down inside on

The village of Conques, opposite, less populous now than it was in the twelfth century, sits on a remote mountainside in the southwestern part of France.

a bench at one of its bare wooden tables and found myself being waited on by a smiling crone, her head wrapped in a shawl and her feet in woolen slippers, who padded up and down the steps between kitchen and dining room with the sure-footedness of a mountain goat. This presumably was la mère Boudou, whom the Grimm brothers would no doubt have identified as Mother Goose's stepsister.

As I sat there watching my breath rise in the heatless chamber, I was reminded of Chaucer's pilgrims, who would have recognized that poor struggling sun skirting the leafless ridge across the way as their own pale-faced Kentish orb.

The colde frosty seson of Decembre. . . .
The bittre frostes, with the sleet and reyn,
Destroyed hath the grene in every yerd.
Janus sit by the fyr, with double berd,
And drinketh of his bugle-horn the wyn.

To be sure, the two bereted yokels who had followed me into la mère Boudou's Merovingian establishment were not exactly double-bearded, and they had left their bugle horns behind; but the determination with which they dipped their mustaches into their wineglasses was unmistakably Chaucerian. No, nothing much had changed hereabouts since the Middle Ages, and Chaucer would have found an admirable subject in the story of Conques, a rollicking medieval tale of pilfering monks and purloined bones.

The first known inhabitant of these wild parts was a pious recluse named

Dadon, who sought refuge here in the latter part of the eighth century. The poor fellow had seen his house sacked and his mother hideously mutilated by the Moors—a spectacle that had confirmed him in the belief that this earth is a vale of tears. He accordingly removed himself to this deserted valley "unknown to man, long repelled by its wild aspect, and the abode of beasts," to quote from an ancient script. The chronicler for once was not exaggerating. This is still a fair description of the Aveyron—or the Rouergue, as it was known in the Middle Ages—which is one of the poorest regions of the Auvergne, in southwestern France. Here the rolling hills and broad green pastures that elsewhere provide some of the choicest beef and butter in France have been compressed into wrinkled valleys. At Conques the ground is so steep that the little town's vegetable patches have been built into escarpments. Terraced vineyards still dot the slopes, though it is now cheaper to buy wine produced in more favored climes. Pork is still the *pièce de résistance* in most humble houses, and only yesterday the chestnuts harvested every autumn from the surrounding woods were used for feeding humans as well as hogs. Which explains why many of Dadon's modern descendants have concluded that there are less painful ways of keeping the wolf from the door than hoeing a few feet of unproductive soil; they have chosen to emigrate, with the curious result that four out of every five barmen and café

By CURTIS CATE

This iron screen in the Conques basilica was made from chains brought to Saint Foy by prisoners she had freed.

owners in Paris today come from this backwoods region.

But in the devout Dadon's day the remoteness of the valley was its saving grace. Word of the good hermit's exemplary devotion eventually got back to the ears of Louis the Pious (later rechristened "the Debonair"), whom Charlemagne, his father, had appointed Duke of Aquitaine. Louis had the holy man brought to him, and after engaging him in lengthy theological discourse he encouraged him to set up a Benedictine abbey in the hitherto uninhabited glen. It was Louis, so posterity claimed, who gave the wild spot the name of Conques (in Latin *concha*), supposedly because it had the shape of a shell (which it doesn't). Founded in 790, the abbey prospered.

Poor the *Auvergnats* may be, but they more than make up for it in guile, as was to be proved once and for all by the crafty monks of Conques. France at this time was in a highly unsettled state, as the pillaging Vikings stormed their way up the Garonne in 850 to sack Toulouse. Encouraged by the Vikings' success, the Moors staged a brief comeback, recrossing the Pyrenees and plundering in their turn. To complete the confusion a wild Mongol host smashed across northern Italy and Provence. Fifty years after his death Charlemagne's empire was a shambles, the barons who should have been defending it being more interested in feuding with each other.

The ultimate beneficiary of this chaos turned out to be the Church, which could at least pose as a disinterested body anxious to limit the damage. But the Church at this time was anything but a unified force. This was an age of *sauve qui peut*, in which each parish had to struggle as best it could to survive. The popes in distant Rome could issue bulls and distribute anathemas, but they did little to meet local needs, which were of a more urgent character. Feudal Europe responded by producing a plethora of saints to fill the void. Jesus Christ, like his vicar in Rome, was no longer enough. Each locality had to have its patron divinity, its own guardian, its *genius loci*—as he would have been known in pagan times—who was simply the religious equivalent of its secular lord.

The French language, amusingly enough, has retained the word "*invention*" to designate the discovery of the sacred relics that each parish had to have in order to claim a saint's protection. Probably the first Frenchman to pull off a major "invention" of this kind was a monk from Fleury called Aigulfe, who journeyed down to Monte Cassino in the year 655 and brought back the bones of Saint Benedict and his sister, Saint Scholastique.

Tours was lucky enough to boast a genuine fifth-century saint—the generous Saint Martin, who had split his cloak with a beggar and who was hon-

ored by the construction of a Romanesque basilica that rose to be the finest church of its day. In Paris the devotees of Saint Denis, its first bishop, had "invented" a wood fragment from the Cross and even several of the nails used to pierce our Saviour's palms and feet. In Autun a local saint called Saint Nazaire was identified with "Lazare" (Lazarus) and was reported to have reached France with his sister, Mary Magdalene. She herself was said to be buried in the vicinity of Aix-en-Provence. This was still too far away for an enterprising Burgundian monk called Badilon, who journeyed down to Aix-en-Provence and brought back the sacred bones to Vézelay. Nîmes could boast the remains of Saint Gilles—notwithstanding a rival claim advanced by the Hungarians, who were too far away and too barbarous to matter. Poitiers had Saint Hilary, and even Angely—a one-horse hamlet if ever there was one—claimed to shelter the venerable head of John the Baptist.

One can imagine the mounting frustration of the friars of Conques as they heard about all these wondrous "inventions" in the bitter realization that their own godforsaken glen had been unhaunted prior to the good Badon's time by anything more glamourous than the footprint of a wolf or the hoot of an owl. The holy fathers set about solving the problem in their own resourceful fashion. To be sure, their first experiment in the genre was not a conspicu-

The tympanum of the Conques basilica is carved with many figures, among them this depiction of Saint Foy in prayer.

ous success. In 855 two monks, Hildebert and Audald, journeyed from Conques to Valencia fired with a zeal to lay hands on the remains of Saint Vincent of Zaragoza. Probably they reckoned that by penetrating this deeply into Moorish territory they could have the theft written off as a piece of infidel sacrilege. They actually got hold of the bones, but on their way back they were ambushed at Zaragoza, the good saint's home town, and forced to relinquish the booty.

Some fifteen more years passed while the monks of Conques gnashed their teeth in helpless wrath. Then, in 870 or thereabouts, another commando force was dispatched to recuperate the bones of another Saint Vincent, buried in the village of Pompéjac, near Agen. The expedition succeeded brilliantly, and the relics were brought safely back to Conques; but to the dismay of the friars the transplanted saint failed to attract the slightest attention.

It was during this raid, however, that the monks first heard of Saint Foy and of the extraordinary miracles that her relics had begun to accomplish in Agen. Located on the banks of the Garonne about eighty miles upstream from Bordeaux, Agen—or Aginum, as it was called by the Romans—had been one of the most important centers of Roman Gaul. Foy, or Fides (to give her her Latin name), was born around A.D. 290, the daughter of a local

patrician who paid homage to the city's Roman gods—Jupiter and Diana; she and her sister were brought up in the Christian faith by their governess. At a very tender age she began to display a deplorable solicitude for the wants of the needy, even going so far as to steal bread from the family kitchen, which she distributed to the poor. Caught red-handed one day by her suspicious father, who wanted to know what it was she was carrying bundled up in a fold of her dress, she had answered: "Flowers!" And lo and behold—for so it is written in the *Liber Miraculorum Sanctae Fidis* (which dates from the eleventh century)—she opened her dress and a cluster of beautiful red flowers flashed forth where the loaf had been.

Fides was just twelve years old when the emperor Diocletian, in the year 303, ordered a ruthless purge of all Christians in the empire. The man sent to Aquitaine to take care of the job was Dacian, the governor of northern Spain, a man for whom orders were orders. In the *Liber Miraculorum Sanctae Fidis* he is depicted as a dark, bloodthirsty horror, but the anonymous author of the *Canczon de Santa Fe* (probably a monk of the eleventh century) portrays him, less harshly, as a kind of subtle scoundrel whose slumbers are troubled, like Pontius Pilate's, by a nagging sense of shame. Here Fides is draped in all the attributes of a heroine in a *chanson de geste:*

Beautiful is her body and small of size,
But fairer still the sense within her.
Lovely are her eyes and white her face . . .

The bard launches into a rapturous description of all the rich things of this world she has fallen heir to but has had the stout Christian courage to disdain:

Great were her lands and castles strong
And furs from wild beasts she had and
 buttons
And on her fingers precious rings,
And plates well made of gold and silver.
All these she fears are evil snares
Wrought for her by the black Devil;
With them she feeds the lepers and the
 poor.
Poor she made herself, like a beggar,
And remained with God, this being
 better.

Such is the radiant creature who is brought before Dacian, the instrument of the abominable Diocletian. The rogue begins by promising her the sun and the moon if she will but renounce Christ and agree to sacrifice to Diana, the city's pagan goddess. He promises her a belt made of gold and "*de vera purpral vestiment*"—a raiment of real crimson. A hundred damsels will wait on her, a thousand cavaliers escort her if only . . . But no, the stouthearted virgin refuses, even going so far as to revile the official gods, who she says are fed a daily diet of toads and perfumed by the hand of the devil in the incense of burning wool. On hearing this outrage *lo mendiz pudolenz* (the

71

stinking wretch—which is to say, Dacian) rolls his eyes and gnashes his teeth. An iron grid is brought forth and a bonfire of walnut trunks is built beneath it. Like Saint Lawrence, Fides is to be roasted alive. At the prospect of this frightful immolation, the people weep and the entire city goes into mourning. But as the flames rise, an angel, white as a dove, comes down from Heaven and, blowing on the fire, puts out the blaze. The angel then places a golden crown on Fides's head and covers her nude body with a gold-spangled robe—though none of this is seen by the Roman governor.

Furious at seeing the blaze dwindle to a heap of tepid ashes, Dacian orders her beheaded. The job is done by the Basques, who drag Fides from the grid and unsheath their swords. One of them, raising his flashing blade, severs her head at a stroke—as Herod did with John the Baptist, adds the poet.

Such was the virgin saint and martyr. Tradition has it that following her glorious death Fides's body, together with that of her sister, was dragged away by the pagans and left to rot beyond the city walls. But the surviving Christians secretly took possession of the truncated bodies, wiping the holy blood off onto pieces of precious cloth —tattered fragments of which later turned up in Saint Foy's reliquary along with locks of hair, bits of jewelry, tiny silk and leather pouches containing cinders, and even bits of blood-stained amianthus. These remains were duly elevated a century later by Saint Dulcidius, Bishop of Agen, who had a tiny brick chapel built to house Fides's marble tomb. Next the sanctuary became a shrine, and later a Benedictine abbey, which is what it was in the second half of the ninth century when the friars of Conques raided the tomb of Saint Vincent de Pompéjac.

Saint Vincent having failed them, the friars of Conques now hatched a scheme for annexing the remains of Saint Foy of Agen. They realized that this was an infinitely more delicate operation and that there was no point in trying a crude frontal assault. As luck would have it there was at hand just the man for the job. His name was Ariviscus, and he was a priest of exemplary piety who in the administration of a neighboring church had displayed "remarkable prudence and a consummate skill in the commerce of life"—which can only mean that he was crafty, taciturn, and tenacious, and thus an *Auvergnat* to the tips of his prayer-joined fingers.

Exchanging his monastic habit for the cloak and staff of a pilgrim, Ariviscus hied himself to Agen with a lay companion and took his time reconnoitering the enemy camp. There was only one word for his performance— masterly. So assiduous was his devotion, so manifest his piety, so simonpure his comportment, so elevated and yet amiable his conversation, that it never occurred to the good monks of Agen that they were admitting a wolf to the fold. They welcomed the newcomer as one of their own and even allowed him to become a guardian of the monastery's prized possessions.

Tradition says that the prudent Ariviscus took ten years to mature his diabolical plan. But even if he only took half that time, his tenacity is awe-inspiring. Having duly taken stock of the habits of his companions, Ariviscus concluded that the most propitious moment for a coup was January 6, the night of the Epiphany. The wintry night would be conveniently long, but even more important, the occasion would be celebrated with an unusually copious dinner, in the course of which even the most vigilant spirits were apt to be numbed by food and drink. And so it happened on this particular Epiphany, in the year 877 (or thereabouts). Excusing himself on the pretext that the abbey's holy relics required a particular watchfulness on this

---

SAINT FOY IN MAJESTY

The statue of Saint Foy opposite, and the other reliquaries kept in the basilica at Conques (three of which appear on the following pages), are among Christianity's most elaborate treasures. Saint Foy dazzles the eye as much as any golden idol of paganism, and fittingly; for in one sense the cult of the martyred virgin of Agen was that of a scarcely disguised pagan goddess. The statue and throne, slightly less than three feet high, are studded with several hundred precious and semiprecious stones —some of them as large as walnuts. And set among the stones there are thirty-one ancient intaglios and two cameos, one of which carries the head of the emperor Caracalla—hardly a lover of Christians—while the other shows the profile of Diana, the Roman goddess to whom Saint Foy refused to sacrifice. The throne is further enhanced with rock-crystal balls, enamels, and silver plaques. The oldest part of the statue is the head, which contains the skull of the martyr. It was fashioned from two sheets of gold in about the fifth century. The body of the statue was created in the ninth century but has since been greatly modified. The tenth century added the crown, the earrings, and the throne; the fourteenth century, the crystal balls; the sixteenth century, the gilded forearms and hands.

Succeeding centuries were hardly so kind to Saint Foy. The cult died out; the village decayed. By the 1920's Conques was in a sad state—its basilica in desperate need of repair and its saint forgotten. A group of private citizens, among them the late Bostonian writer and scholar Henry Copley Greene, set about collecting funds and making restorations. Today Conques is one of the loveliest, if least known, of France's historic churches.

OVERLEAF: The icy blue eyes in this detail belie Saint Foy's reputation as *sancta joculatrix*—the prankish saint. Bernard of Antwerp, a twelfth-century priest who once stared into these orbs, took the statue for a pagan idol and recoiled. Later he succumbed to their spell and wrote the first chronicle of her miracles.

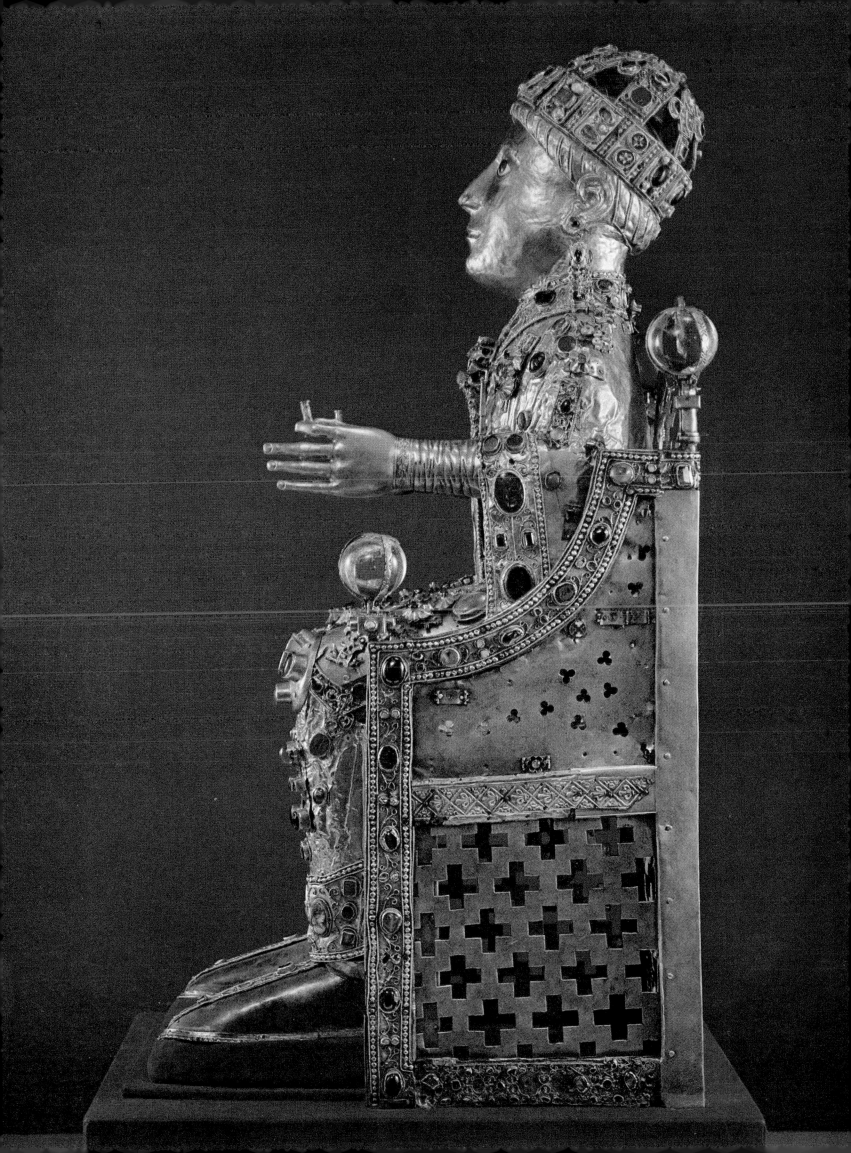

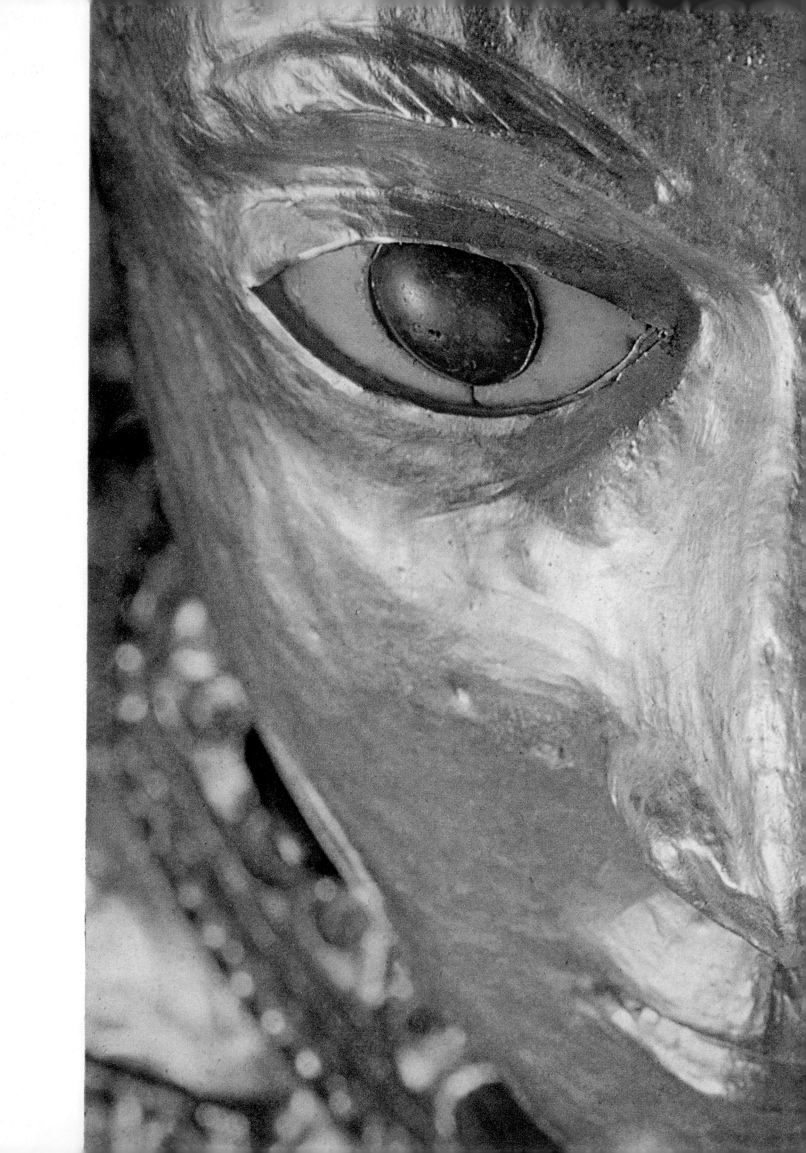

Pepin's reliquary, so called for reasons now forgotten, is adorned with precious stones and filigree work surrounding a figure of the crucified Christ between John and the Virgin Mary. The chest was made circa 1000, presumably to contain the foreskin of Christ.

festive night—a gesture of self-sacrifice that won him the enthusiastic acclaim of his colleagues—Ariviscus quietly repaired to the chapel. Unable to lift the marble slab covering the saint's remains, Ariviscus calmly took a crowbar and a hammer and smashed open a hole at the foot of the tomb. He then dragged out Saint Foy's bones, slipped them into a large potato sack, and stole out of the abbey while his fellow monks continued to carouse.

What must have been their dismay the next morning on entering the chapel to find—oh, horror of hor-

rors—the tomb of their revered saint desecrated! The sudden absence of the devout Ariviscus made it clear who the miscreant had been, but the flabbergasted monks lost a number of precious hours vainly wringing their hands and wondering what to do. Saint Foy was not only their saint but also a patron of Agen, and loud and bitter were the recriminations when the dreadful tidings swept through town.

A few horsemen were hastily assembled and sent after the blackguard. They succeeded only in getting lost. A new expedition was forthwith pre-

pared, and this time the riders actually caught up with the villain at the village of Lalbenque, near Cahors. Ariviscus and his companion were resting under a large tree when the horsemen trotted up and asked if by any chance they had seen an absconding monk pass that way. They described the abominable scoundrel in full, dark detail, and the trembling Ariviscus had barely enough courage to answer no, neither he nor his companion had seen the rogue. His disguise—probably a wig and certainly a hat to conceal his tonsured pate—luckily fooled his pursuers. The medieval chronicle ascribes this narrow escape to "divine protection."

The horsemen then rode on to Conques, where they were greeted with expressions of bland surprise. What? The bones of Saint Foy had been stolen from Agen by a monk called Ariviscus? Heavens, what was the world coming to? No, they hadn't seen him and hadn't the slightest idea what had become of him. Years had passed since he had vanished from these parts. Fatigued and dispirited, the horsemen turned about and rode sadly back to Agen. Here again one can detect the masterly touch of the shrewd *Auvergnat* friar. Instead of making straight for Conques, Ariviscus had decided to take his time and return by a deliberately circuitous route.

Loud was the rejoicing when the two tired travelers finally heaved into Conques with their treasure. It was the fourteenth of January, eight days after the coup had been pulled off. For centuries thereafter this date was celebrated as the beginning of the golden age of Conques.

For from that moment the fortunes of this backwoods valley changed. The first to benefit from Saint Foy's magic touch was a former steward named Guibert, who had had his eyes torn out during a violent altercation with his master, a local landlord called Géraud. Forced to choose another form of livelihood, Guibert had ended up a *badin*, which is to say, a wandering storyteller and entertainer. On the eve of her feast day, now celebrated on October 6, Saint Foy appeared to him and promised that if he made the pilgrimage to Conques and lit two candles—one for the altar of the Saviour, the other for her tomb—he would recover his sight. In his home village of Espeyrac, situated on the uplands east of Conques, his description of his vision was greeted as the hallucinatory raving of a madman. But Guibert finally managed to pry a few coins out of a neighbor to buy the candles. He lit them as instructed and prostrated himself in front of the saint's relics. By and by he saw, as though in a daze, two shining globules the size of olives descend from on high and fix themselves in his eye sockets, and when he awoke the next morning, he was startled to *see* the church full of candles lit for the celebration of matins.

News of this miracle spread over the countryside, attracting a host of pilgrims from near and far. The abbot, who knew a good thing when he saw one, gave Guibert a job as a wax salesman, and soon not only Saint Foy but the fortunate Guibert himself was being showered with presents by persons hoping to be healed by the saint. Fame went to Guibert's head, and finally, to put a curb on his boasting, Saint Foy was forced to reimpose his blindness. After a few months of darkness he was readmitted to the light, only to be deprived of it again when he reverted to his braggart ways. No one was quite sure whether he was blessed or mad, but nothing could dim the prestige of this "*illuminé*," as he was called, and of the saint who had given him back his sight.

The significance of the tale is unmistakable. Behind it one can detect that struggle between the rational and the irrational that rent the Church throughout the Middle Ages. But the moral is not simply that the inner light of faith is more precious than the outer, and that a blind man can regain his sight if he concentrates on God and walks in the way of the Lord. The story alludes to the elevation that may be granted to a *badin* who will place his talents as an entertainer at the disposal of God. The *badin* was first cousin to the jongleur, who was part acrobat, part juggler, part mime, part bard, part storyteller, and as often as not a lute player as well, and who haunted not only the courts but the porches of the churches. In a largely illiterate age the minstrels were as influential as the monks in educating the common herd, regaling their audiences with the heroic exploits of King Arthur and Lancelot and Roland and the rest. They entertained pilgrims all over France and over vast areas of Europe, and just as they helped kindle the fervor of those who were undertaking the pilgrimage to Santiago de Compostela in Spain, so it was they who more than any others were to spread the fame of Saint Foy across the length and breadth of Christendom.

Giving sight to the blind became one of the special virtues of the saint, and her cult in the eleventh, twelfth, and thirteenth centuries can only be compared with that of Our Lady of Lourdes in our own time. The waters of the Auvergne have long been noted for their health-giving properties, and the cult of Saint Foy at Conques was encouraged by the purity of the mountain spring that continues to bubble forth not far from the basilica's southern tower.

To house the saint's skull a special gold statue was wrought and embossed with a fabulous quantity of precious stones and antique cameos. These came from pious "donations," which the gentle saint was particularly resourceful in extracting. The abbot of Beaulieu was so hounded by a series of visions that he finally agreed to part with two beautiful gold doves, which went to embellish her throne. Arsinde, the barren wife of Guillaume Taillefer, Count of Toulouse, who finally consented to part with two precious bracelets, was rewarded with two sons in exchange. When Countess Richarde, the wife of Raymond III, Count of Rouergue, refused to give up a gold brooch, Saint Foy punished her by causing her horse to rear and the brooch to get caught on a branch. A few days later it was brought to the abbey by a pious woman of the neighborhood who had found it.

Saint Foy's ingenuity in circumventing the wiles of avarice soon won her the title of *sancta joculatrix*—the prankish saint. For a while she swept all before her, and from Rouergue her fame spread over a good part of the Auvergne. Soon Conques was besieged with requests to have the miraculous

This reliquary is called Charlemagne's "A," but the attribution is legendary. It was made in the eleventh century to hold what may have been a piece of Saint Foy's dress.

statue brought over to bless this or that community. Such outings were almost invariably attended by miracles, each miracle necessitating the celebration of a special mass to the repeated flourish of trumpets and the ceaseless pealing of bells. On one of her more memorable excursions—to the town of Molompise, which lies in the heart of the Auvergne—the miracles, falling almost as thickly as snowflakes, kept the hard-pressed monks of Conques from having time to eat anything for more than twenty-four hours.

For such occasions the statue, preceded by a jewel-studded cross, would usually be placed on a richly caparisoned horse, though she was also carried at times on a tapestried litter. Torches and candles accompanied her, joyously clashing cymbals heralded her triumphant approach as well as the deep-throated sound of oliphants—horns hollowed out of elephants' tusks. No instrument was more prized in the Middle Ages, at any rate by knights and crusaders. It was on an oliphant that Roland blew the final heroic blast, heard for thirty leagues around, that informed Charlemagne that his rearguard was in trouble.

Conques was a stopping point on one of the four major pilgrimage routes to Santiago de Compostela, and the same martial fervor that made this for a while the greatest pilgrimage in Europe can be detected in another facet of Saint Foy's miracle-working powers. She was responsible for miraculously freeing an extraordinary number of prisoners, who then brought their locks and their chains to Conques as a token of their homage. In all probability many of these "miraculous" escapes were organized by resourceful prelates. The fathers of the Church, who were no fools, recognized what was demonstrated once again during the last war—that former criminals and jailbirds make excellent commandos and singularly resourceful soldiers, whom the Church needed for the pilgrimage to Santiago and to fight the Moors in Spain. The banner they fought under was the banner of Saint James—Sant Iago—transmuted from a humble Galilean pedestrian into a sword-wielding horseman, the blood brother of el Cid Campeador.

They also fought under another banner—that of Santa Fe, to give her her Spanish and Provençal name. For as her fame grew, so did the requests for her remains. A church was founded in her honor in Alsace; a priory was dedicated to her in Bavaria, and another sprang up in Liège; several churches were built for her in Italy; and even London acquired a chapel established in her honor. But it was in Spain, where half a dozen churches were dedicated to her, that her fame was greatest. It was she whose aid Raymond III, Count of Rouergue, invoked in liberating Barcelona from the Saracens in the year 987. It was again she who aided Don Pedro Sanchez, the king of Aragon, in chasing the Moors from his kingdom. The memory of these exploits was still very much alive centuries later when the conquistadors crossed the Atlantic, and the Spanish mission fathers once again invoked her help in combating a new kind of infidel—one with a red skin and war paint—as they did at Santa Fe, in what came to be known as New Mexico.

At its height—in the eleventh and twelfth centuries—Conques' abbey numbered close to nine hundred monks, or almost twice the total population of present-day Conques. They were spread for leagues around, tilling the fields and sowing wheat on the uplands above the valley or milling flour

One of the treasures of Conques is this golden arm, supposedly containing a bone of Saint George the dragon slayer.

down at the old mill (which still exists) a mile or two upstream on the Dordou river. Artisans were imported by the muleload and were kept busy for decades fashioning gold and silver and other precious metals into fabulous new reliquaries. Two new basilicas had to be built as each grew too small to contain the host of pilgrims who came to pay homage to the priceless gold statue of the saint. The hundreds of chains and locks brought to her by escaped prisoners were melted down and reworked into a series of beautiful forged-iron gates and grills, which now surround the pillars of the apse. In the Middle Ages they were used to protect the gold statue and the other treasures of Conques, which were kept on more or less permanent display; the church at night was a sea of candles as scores of pilgrims spent night-long wakes guarding the precious treasure from lurking thieves.

And then, almost as suddenly as it had flared, the cult burned itself out. By 1424 there were only twenty-nine monks left. A century later a pontifical decree turned the abbey into a secular church. In the 1590's the basilica narrowly missed destruction when the Protestants marched up and set fire to the roof; but fortunately they spared the treasure. The revolutionaries who marched up the valley two centuries later were bent on demolishing the treasures, but the resourceful spirit of Ariviscus was still very much alive among these backward yokels, who got advance warning of what was brewing down below. They hastily removed the treasures from the church and buried them, then smashed a couple of locks, bent a few iron bars, and left open one of the grillwork gates. When the rabble marched up the hill, they were greeted by some glum-faced locals who stared at them woodenly before breaking the terrible news: they had been beaten to the spot by a bunch of godless bandits who had broken into the sanctuary and decamped with the loot!

For years there was not a house or a cabbage patch in Conques that did not have some priceless piece of jewelry buried away beneath it, yet such was the continuing faith in their guardian patroness and saint that not one of these religious heirlooms disappeared. One by one they crept back into the basilica as the memory of Robespierre's Terror faded into the past. Today they are housed in a specially constructed wing of the cloister behind panels of protective glass. They constitute the finest collection of Carolingian art in France; and as one descends into the darkened crypt where they repose, one has the impression of having suddenly stumbled into some magic cavern ablaze with the marvels of Aladdin's lamp.

For major feast days the statue is still solemnly brought out, placed on a simple litter, and paraded up the village's one and only tarred street. The procession winds past the timbered façade of the Auberge de Sainte-Foy and on up to a kind of square, shaded by a fine old chestnut. The bells peal, but there are no oliphants any more to fill the echoing valley with the sound of Roland's horn. Gone, too, are the lutes and the split-reed pipes with which the jongleurs of the Middle Ages used to amuse the pilgrims gathered on the cobbles in front of the basilica.

History has passed Conques by. In a sense it is a blessing.

Curtis Cate, for years the European editor of the Atlantic-Monthly, *is an American free-lance writer now living in Paris. He is currently at work on a biography of Saint-Exupéry.*

The Wars of the Roses

"*Like modern gang warfare, the Wars of the Roses*

were no mere social aberrations;

they were the ugly sign of a society gone wrong . . .

where the son found it necessary

to warn his mother to lock her doors not only at night

but also during the daytime"

By LACEY BALDWIN SMITH

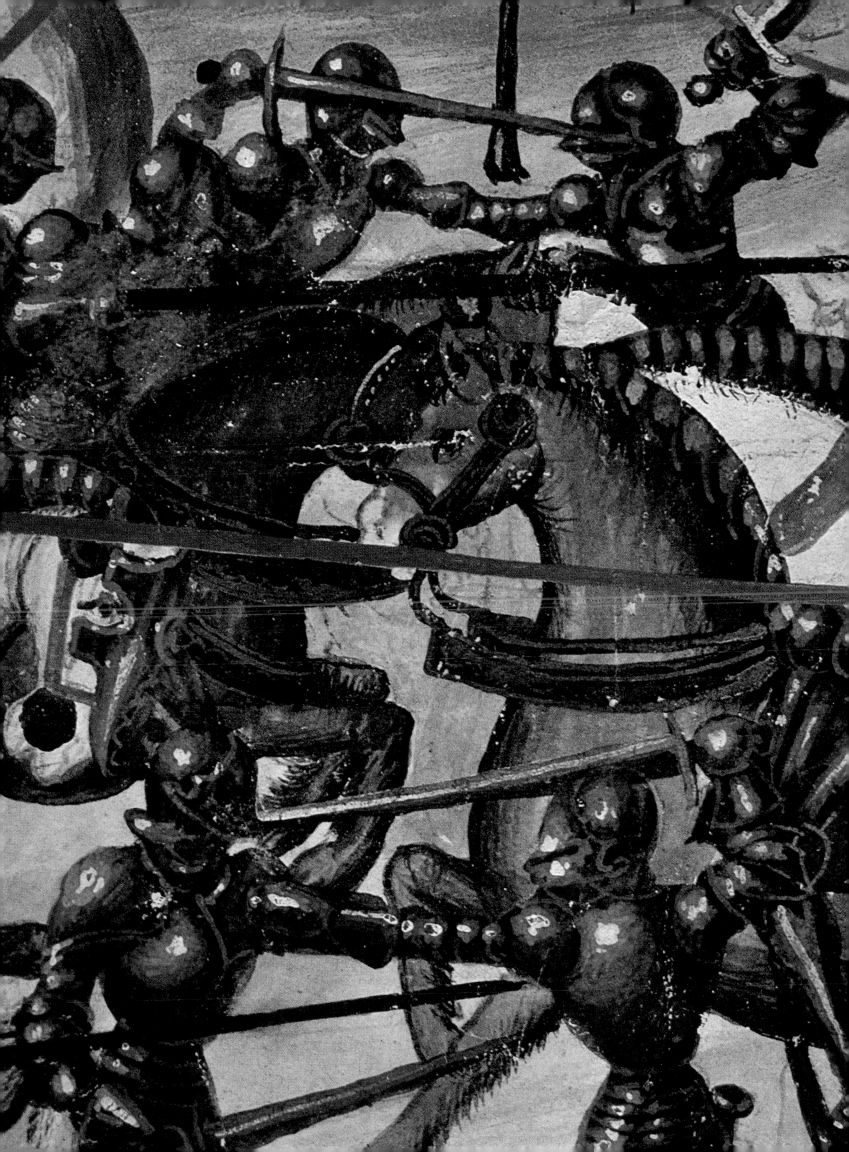

or anyone who has had to suffer through textbook and monograph the Wars of the Roses are prime examples of the horrors of studying history, especially late medieval history. Out of the welter of yellow parchments, faded heraldic colors, and a good deal of misnamed floral symbolism emerge only puzzlement as to what it was all about and a general sense of confusion in which kings persist in getting out of order, barons keep changing their names or allegiances, and students are never quite sure whether Henry VI, Part II refers to a Shakespearean play or a division of the reign. Almost in self-defense the reader seeks to impose romantic order upon historical chaos by viewing the commotion as a well-bred and peculiarly English affair in which a Lancastrian lion and a Yorkist falcon pranced up and down the kingdom competing noisily but ineffectually for the crown. Knights sought to test their military prowess and chivalric ardor in skirmishes invariably fought in the fog and snow, or they galloped about the realm protecting the poor, chastising the wicked, and saving fair damsels from various fates worse than death. The problem for the professional historian is not how to debunk this kind of legend, but how to make intelligible a series of gang wars in which the ringleaders, instead of having such suitable names as Dutch Jake or Reno Starkey, were princes, dukes, and lords.

To do so, kings and battles must be allowed to recede into the mist of history while the spotlight is focused on the social and emotional bonds that held society together. Fifteenth-century England was staggering under a triple shock—a rising tide of violence that swept the kingdom to the edge of anarchy, a narrowing spiral of economic contraction that turned moderate squires into militant henchmen, and the curse of disputed succession that converted the crown into a political football. Like modern gang warfare,

the Wars of the Roses were no mere social aberrations; they were the ugly sign of a society gone wrong, of a world where the traitor was not simply executed but was axed with a rusty sword, where the brigand no longer stole but slew his victim horribly and spoiled him "unto the naked skin," and where the son found it necessary to warn his mother to lock her doors not only at night but also during the daytime for fear of thieves who rode "with great fellowships like lords."

Violence is difficult to judge, either quantitatively or qualitatively; so much depends on society's level of tolerance to pain, suffering, and animal brutality. Simple lawlessness and delight in mayhem were inherent in a civilization that made a virtue of fighting, glorified the warrior's code of bravery and loyalty, and accepted as the major pastime of the ruling elite the mock warfare of the joust. Though the priest and the scholar sought to model society in their own images, there was no doubt where the really important people stood. "By God's body," exclaimed one nobleman, "I had rather that my son should hang than study Latin! For it becomes the sons of gentlemen to blow the hunting horn well, to hunt skillfully, and ele-

A Note About the Roses

As if the wars themselves were not sufficiently confusing, the very name given to them is suspect. The heraldic symbols of the red and the white roses were never used by the actual combatants. The white rose was merely one of York's lesser devices; the red rose, though a Lancastrian badge, was never worn by Henry VI. Shakespeare, in the famous Temple Garden scene of *Henry VI, Part I*, Act II, Scene 4, immortalized the symbols largely because the Tudors had made the contrasting colors the center of their escutcheon. The term "Wars of the Roses" is of even more recent origin, appearing first in Sir Walter Scott's *Anne of Geierstein*, (1829).

gantly to carry and train the hawk." The Middle Ages was permeated with a kind of frontier spirit—a profound respect for the principles of law, but an acute dislike and distrust of all law-enforcing agencies—and the statistics of Lincolnshire in the thirteenth century, where over three hundred crimes of violence were committed in a single year, is evidence enough that society had but small regard for the contemplative life.

Baronial feuding was endemic throughout Europe, and compared to other ages and kingdoms, the thirteen weeks of campaigning during the Wars of the Roses—thirteen weeks in thirty-two years—seems ludicrously small. The problem was not a matter of degree but of kind: it was an increase of violence in that element of society responsible for law enforcement. Brutality was becoming a habit among the ruling classes when a man such as Thomas Foljambe, in retaliation for a murderous assault two years before, attacked and mutilated Sir Henry Pierpoint while he was attending a church service. The king's law had little meaning when in 1454 a royal courier sent to arrest Sir Nicholas Longford of Derbyshire for having viciously assailed Sir Thomas Blount was set upon by a band of Sir Nicholas's servants, who tried to force the royal writ down the messenger's throat. The prospect was scarcely appetizing, since the document consisted of sixty square inches of parchment and a privy seal two and a half inches in diameter.

Humiliation and indigestion on the part of the king's courier might be dismissed as a healthy example of feudal independence and frontier disinclination to introduce public law into pri-

The last "pure" Plantagenet, Richard II, opposite, surrendered his crown to the bold Lancastrian usurper Henry Bolingbroke, who became Henry IV, in 1399. Richard's abdication set off royal turmoil that raged for more than eighty years. This detail is taken from a contemporary manuscript of the Chronicles of Froissart.

A joust

Battling at close quarters, c. 1400

Scenes of war and violence in the era of the Wars of the Roses are shown here as contemporaries depicted them. In one regard the artists of the day mislead: the age of knightly combat on rearing chargers was well on the wane, and combatants now fought mainly on foot. At that, archers, opposite at far right, outnumbered the heavily armored knights by as much as ten to one in the armies of the time.

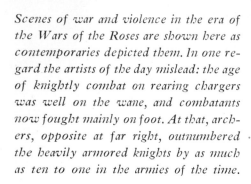
Dragging a captive to his execution, c. 1440

vate matters had it not been that the Longfords and Blounts of medieval society were motivated by something far more dangerous than simple relish for murder and mutilation. Behind family violence stood a desperate war of economic and political survival.

Like the poor, the economic determinist is always with us, and it is hard to counter his argument that the root of social and political evil in the fifteenth century must be sought in the diminishing revenues of the governing class. As France bled to death during the second half of the Hundred Years' War, the entire European economy began to shrink, and the English landlords and merchants, though temporarily sustained by the plunder of war, eventually felt the pinch. To the devastation of battle was added the horror of plague, which struck in 1348, ravaging the European population for the next fifty years and casting a third to a half of Christendom into nameless communal graves. Throughout England there were fewer mouths to feed, fewer backs to cover, fewer luxuries to satisfy, and fewer peasants to till the soil. Land surplus and labor shortage, with their corollaries of high wages and low rents, spelled financial ruin unless the landed classes could supplement their incomes from the profits of dynastic war, ferocious litigation, and political gangsterism.

During the economic crisis the ruling elite did what came most naturally: they emphasized those elements of feudalism that could be distorted and manipulated to increase their revenues and sustain their positions. The great magnates used their prestige to build up political-military followings and forced their way into the king's council, where they breathed self-interested advice into the sovereign's ear and manipulated royal finance and justice to benefit themselves and their followers. As one contemporary put it, the great lords were so occupied with concern for "their kin, servants and tenants that they attended but little to the King's matter." The lesser landholders turned instinctively to the men above them and offered military service in return for a fixed salary, or simply accepted a great baron's livery, looking to him for what the fifteenth century called good lordship.

Lordship was the central political and psychological bond holding feudal society together, but at the same time it was the source of much of the social evil of the day. Lordship was built into the contractual relationship whereby a lord granted land to his vassal in return for service, and it was the essential formula by which a man could be known and described. Feudal society asked, not an individual's nationality, but the name of his overlord. Today a citizen without a country is a contradiction in terms; in medieval England a man without a lord was lost, a wanderer without status or defense. If knight and squire were well advised to find themselves a good lord, my

Besieging a castle with a mortar and cannon, c. 1460

Archers at Tewkesbury, 1471

Soldiers pillaging a house

lord's honor and reputation were in direct proportion to the number of dependents who sat at his banquet table or wore his livery. As Mr. John Paston of Norfolk noted, "men do not lure hawks with empty hands," and a great baron was expected to support those who displayed his badge by making their quarrels his own. The arrangement of good lordship was mutually advantageous; the lord maintained his followers in their law suits, bribing the judge and intimidating the jury; he lent them armed support in their feuds, avenging their injuries and chastising their enemies; and he exercised his patronage in their quest for office. In return they guaranteed him control over the instruments of political influence: the machinery of local government and justice. Lord William Hastings, for instance, was careful to select his friends and retainers not only from the landed elements who needed his political and economic support, but also from those who could do him the most good in the shires. Of the ninety men who legally owed him service, twenty were landed gentlemen, fifty-nine were esquires, nine were knights, and two were peers of the realm; and of this number some twenty were sheriffs of the shires, and thirty-three were justices of the peace.

Lordship may have offered protection to men of lesser social position, and dignity to the rich and mighty, but it also lay at the root of most of the distortion and injustice in society. It placed in the hands of unruly and economically desperate landholders instruments of violence that far exceeded their individual abilities to subvert law and order. It also made it likely that any petty squabble could mushroom into a conflict involving the honor and interests of the politically powerful. A case in point is the behavior of Sir William Tailboys of Lincolnshire, who was at odds, for reasons unknown, with Sir Hugh Wytham of Boston. The quarrel may have concerned land, injured pride, or the sheer pleasure of feuding, but whatever the cause, Sir Hugh thoroughly thrashed and then imprisoned one of Tailboys's servants. Outraged, Sir William called upon his good lord Viscount Beaumont to order out his retainers and rescue the man. Wytham in turn appealed to his patron Lord Welles, who obligingly transferred the unfortunate creature from a Boston jail to his private castle and threatened to hang him. Behind Beaumont and Welles loomed even greater figures, the dukes of Suffolk and York, who could be called upon to exercise their good lordships, thereby transforming a Boston street brawl into a national incident directly involving members of the king's council.

The dangers of good lordship might have been limited to the more backward and isolated shires had the system operated only from the bottom up. What eventually destroyed the last vestiges of social cohesion was not the petty squabbles of men like Tailboys

85

and Wytham, but the pride and wilfulness of the great magnates themselves. The obligation whereby lesser men were committed to take the "full part and quarrel" of their lord "against all persons, save the King" meant that fear and hatred at the top could at any moment erupt into anarchy at the bottom. Whole counties could be turned into "dens of wolves": in Devonshire the Earl of Devon and Lord William Bonville indulged in a private war that reached new peaks of violence and shocked even a century stained in blood and accustomed to bad faith and outrage.

Thomas Courtenay, twelfth Earl of Devon, was a particularly proud but impecunious nobleman whose ancient lineage was insufficient solace for an income of barely a thousand pounds a year. The Courtenays were the traditional leaders of Devonshire society, and they looked with the darkest suspicion upon the pretensions of the Bonvilles of Shute, a respectable but ambitious clan whose growing influence in local government was threatening what the Courtenays considered to be their birthright. Hostility between the two families came to a head over the stewardship of the crown lands of Cornwall. In 1437 Sir William Bonville

was appointed steward, an office that the Courtenays had regarded as a hereditary perquisite. Three years later Devon was able to have the decision reversed, and private war broke out. For fourteen years the infection spread upward through the web of interlocking lordships until it reached the very top, amalgamating with the dynastic rivalry between the houses of York and Lancaster. On the national level a personal struggle for control of the king's council between the royal cousins Richard, Duke of York, and the Lancastrian Duke of Somerset was polarizing a host of local hatreds into two vast systems of lordship, capable of engulfing the kingdom in civil war if ever either leader determined on liquidating his political rival by force of arms. The Bonvilles enlisted the support of the Earl of Wiltshire and the Duke of Somerset, while Devon turned to Lord Cobham and eventually to Richard, Duke of York. When Somerset and the Lancastrians were in power at court, Bonville received a peerage and had his stewardship reconfirmed, but in March of 1454 the tables were turned when York was created Lord Protector of the Realm. Almost immediately Devon had his revenge when his son Thomas Courtenay committed

A Tangled, Bloodstained Lineage

The chart at the right summarizes the tangled line of succession to the English throne that was both cause and effect of the Wars of the Roses. After the death of the Plantagenet king Edward III four houses contributed kings to the throne in a line of succession that begins, on the chart, at the upper left. Each of the houses could trace some kind of descent from Edward. The Plantagenet Richard II was Edward III's grandson. The Lancastrians, who usurped Richard's throne, claimed descent from Edward's third son, John of Gaunt. Their rivals and successors, the Yorkists, had a clearer claim, having descended both from Edward's fourth son, Edmund of Langley, and, through marriage, from his second son, Lionel of Antwerp. The peacemaking Tudor dynasty had, genealogically, the weakest claim of all, having been formed through two illicit unions, which are indicated on the chart by dotted lines. The first was that between John of Gaunt and his mistress Catherine Swynford, later his third wife, which produced the Beaufort house. The second was the union between Henry V's consort, Catherine of Valois, and her Welsh lover Owen Tudor. Their son married a Beaufort, and their grandson acceded to the throne as Henry VII. On the chart each king is represented by an approximately contemporary portrait.

Lionel
of Antwerp
Duke of Claren
d. 1368

Philippa
m. Edmund Mort

Roger Mortime
d. 1398

Anne Mortime
m. Richard
Earl of Cambrid

LEGEND

Strips of pale color indicate the various royal houses descended from Edward III. The ribbon of bold colors traces the line of succession to the throne and indicates the house to which each king belonged.

LANCASTER	YORK
PLANTAGENET	BEAUFORT
TUDOR	MORTIMER
SLAIN IN BATTLE	MURDERED
SUICIDE	EXECUTED

ILLEGITIMATE UNION

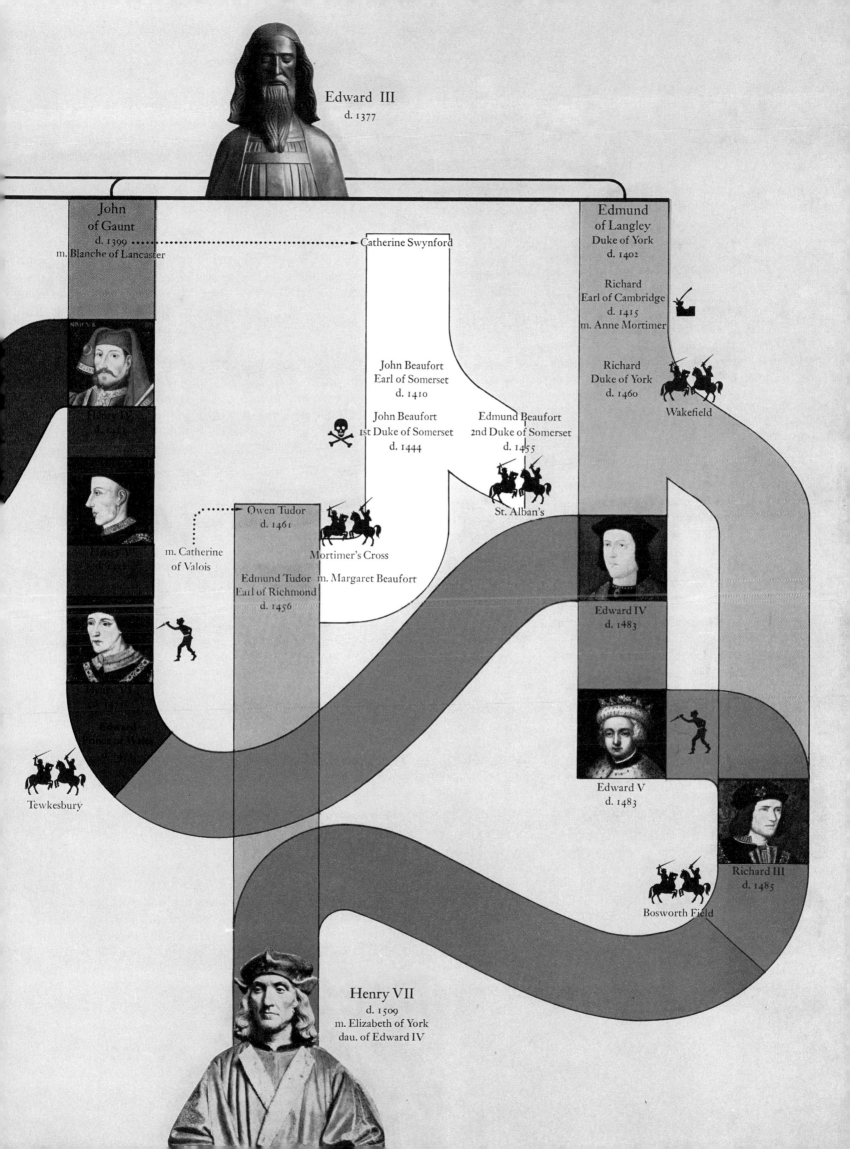

Edward III
d. 1377

John
of Gaunt
d. 1399
m. Blanche of Lancaster

Catherine Swynford

Edmund
of Langley
Duke of York
d. 1402

Richard
Earl of Cambridge
d. 1415
m. Anne Mortimer

John Beaufort
Earl of Somerset
d. 1410

Richard
Duke of York
d. 1460

Wakefield

John Beaufort
1st Duke of Somerset
d. 1444

Edmund Beaufort
2nd Duke of Somerset
d. 1455

St. Alban's

Owen Tudor
d. 1461

Mortimer's Cross

m. Catherine
of Valois

Edmund Tudor m. Margaret Beaufort
Earl of Richmond
d. 1456

Edward IV
d. 1483

Edward V
d. 1483

Tewkesbury

Richard III
d. 1485

Bosworth Field

Henry VII
d. 1509
m. Elizabeth of York
dau. of Edward IV

the most notorious private outrage of the century, a crime unusual for its premeditation, bad faith, and viciousness, for it struck at Lord Bonville through one of his more innocent retainers.

Sir Nicholas Radford of Upcott was an elderly gentleman, a knight of the shire, a lawyer of great local reputation, and a close friend of Lord Bonville's. On the evening of Thursday, October 23, Devon's son assembled over a hundred of his father's henchmen and surrounded Radford's manor house. To gain entry, he perjured his honor as a "true knight and gentleman," swearing on his "faith and truth" that Sir Nicholas would "suffer no bodily harm" nor damage to his property. Once he was inside, the house was looted, the chapel was stripped bare, and the stables were swept clean. Even Sir Nicholas's wife, "sore sick" for two years, was unceremoniously rolled out of bed, and "the sheets that she lay in" were pilfered. When young Courtenay demanded that Radford accompany him back to his father's castle, Sir Nicholas bitterly lamented "Oh, Sir Thomas Courtenay, you have broken your promise. I am old and feeble and can hardly travel on foot, so I must beg of you to be allowed to ride." "No force, Radford," Courtenay answered, "thou shalt ride enough anon, and therefore come on with me." No more than a stone's throw from the house the old man was struck down, and as the earl's son rode away shouting over his shoulder "Farewell, Radford," the young lord's three personal servants dispatched Sir Nicholas with singular brutality. One hacked at his head till the brains fell out, another cut his throat, and the third drove a dagger into his heart; and so was Sir Nicholas Radford "feloniously and horribly slain and murdered."

On the following Monday Devon himself lent his full support to his son's action; with total disdain for justice, he sent his men back to Upcott chapel, where Radford's corpse lay in state, with orders to stage a mock inquest and to bring in a verdict of suicide. To complete the indecency they pitched the body out of its coffin, stripped it of its shroud, and dumped it naked into a pit. Then, "having no more compassion nor pity than though it had been a Jew or a Saracen," they horribly smashed the head and torso beyond recognition by casting into the grave the stones that Sir Nicholas himself had gathered for his tomb.

For six years Courtenay and Bonville turned Devonshire into a battlefield in which local hatreds were more meaningful than party labels. During the dynastic struggle between the houses of York and Lancaster both men switched sides, and their feuding only ended with death in the carnage of the nobility known to history as the Wars of the Roses. Bonville received no mercy from his old enemy the Earl of Devon, who insisted on his execution when the Yorkists were defeated on February 17, 1461, at the second battle of St. Albans. Lord Bonville's son and grandson were already dead, having been killed the previous December at Wakefield, where Richard, Duke of York, himself had been slain. The Earl of Devon died of natural causes, but retribution eventually descended upon his son Thomas, who was captured and beheaded when the Lancastrian nobility was routed at Towton in March of 1461. In Lincolnshire the same butchery of the gentry took place. Sir William Tailboys died in 1464 during one of the final skirmishes of the wars. He had been found hiding in a coal pit, and since "he had much money with him, both gold and silver," there was a double reason for murder: he was both rich and a Lancastrian.

The urge for personal and immediate advantage at the expense of ultimate social gain, and the compulsion to spill blood in the name of family honor were partly social reflexes, partly the result of a contracting economy, and partly the consequence of overlapping good lordships; but the element that converted mere disorder into organized civil war was the curse of disputed succession. Up to this point the story of medieval England gone wrong has been one of institutional perversion and social and political distortion; it now must be presented in terms of the personal ambitions of men who were reaching for the crown. As Shakespeare knew, if the stage of war is to assume proper dramatic proportions, it must not be littered with the minor tragedies of Tailboyses, Courtenays, Longfords, Foljambes, and Radfords but with "sad stories of the death of kings"—and it is in 1399–1400, with the murder of Richard II and the seizure of his throne by Henry Bolingbroke, Duke of Lancaster, that both poet and professional historian begin their explanation for the Wars of the Roses.

Richard II was the last of the undisputed Plantagenet monarchs, for his royal descent was unimpeachable: his father was Edward III's eldest son, the Black Prince. Purity of blood, however, was no substitute for political tact and cunning, and Richard eventually earned a reputation as a tyrant. The act that precipitated his fall was the decision to deny his first cousin Henry Bolingbroke his legal inheritance as the son and heir of John of Gaunt, Duke of Lancaster, Edward III's third surviving son (see chart, pages 86–87). By ignoring his cousin's rights Richard transformed Bolingbroke from a traitor into a justly aggrieved subject who successfully called upon the support of all men seeking to safeguard their estates and titles from the caprice of arbitrary kingship. The king was forced to abdicate in favor of Bolingbroke, who mounted the throne as Henry IV on October 13, 1399. In three months Richard was dead, murdered under circumstances that still remain in doubt.

For Shakespeare the issue was a moral one, involving a vassal's duty to his lord and the divinity that "doth hedge a king." No matter how righteous Bolingbroke's cause in defending his right to inherit the dukedom of

Lancaster, no human justice could wash clean the "heinous, black, obscene" crime of slaying God's royal captain and chosen deputy. The Lancastrian line was tainted at its source, and not even the hero-king Henry V, as he waited for God's decision on the eve of Agincourt, where a tiny band of Englishmen was to butcher an immense French army, could escape the heavy burden of guilt.

O God of battles! steel my soldiers' hearts;
Possess them not with fear; take from them now
The sense of reckoning, if the opposed numbers
Pluck their hearts from them. Not today, O Lord!
O! not today, think not upon the fault
My father made in compassing the crown.

For the victor of Agincourt God withheld his hand, but the sins of the grandfather were visited on the grandson, a babe of nine months when he ascended the dual thrones of England and France in 1422. With singular perversity Henry VI, England's most

saintly sovereign, became the vehicle through which the terrible prophecy was revealed:

And if you crown him, let me prophesy,
The blood of English shall manure the ground
And future ages groan for this foul act;
Peace shall go to sleep with Turks and infidels,
And in this seat of peace tumultuous wars
Shall kin with kin and kind with kind confound;
Disorder, horror, fear and mutiny
Shall here inhabit, and this land be call'd
The field of Golgotha and dead man's skulls.
O! if you raise this house against this house,
It will the woefullest division prove
That ever fell upon this cursed earth.
Prevent it, resist it, let it not be so,
Lest child, child's children, cry against you 'woe!'

Modern historians are somewhat less convinced than was Shakespeare of

At the court of Henry VI, the weak king is shown surrounded by sycophants in a 1443 manuscript illumination. Many of his courtiers soon emerged as the schemers of the Yorkist and Lancastrian parties.

divine interference, but they are equally willing to begin the Wars of the Roses with the dire consequences of Richard's death; for the year 1399 marked a fateful break in the traditional succession of the crown from eldest son to eldest son. Once the succession was broken, the throne was exposed to the claim of almost anyone who could manufacture a descent from that source of all fifteenth-century genealogical and dynastic troubles —the many sons of Edward III. The moment the unimpeachable right of Richard II as Edward's lawful heir through his eldest son was replaced by the highly tenuous claims of Henry IV, a giant stride was taken in the war of might versus right. Henceforth any one of a multitude of contending Plantagenet cousins had a perfectly valid claim to the English crown. It merely depended on who was the mightiest. While Henrys IV and V lived, the danger lay hidden; but the moment Lancastrian leadership faltered in 1422 and a nine-month-old baby, who grew into a virtuous if incompetent sovereign, mounted the throne, the stage was set for a tragedy that eventually cost the lives of three English kings and countless descendants of Edward III.

By 1450 almost thirty years of minority government, intrafamily bickering, and administrative ineptitude had so paralyzed royal leadership that men began to turn to the most important of all the Plantagenet cousins, Richard, Duke of York. The duke possessed a dangerous rival ancestry. He could trace his lineage back to two of Edward III's sons, and he could even argue that in strictly legal terms his pedigree was more valid than that of the king, whose Plantagenet blood came from the third surviving son of Edward III. York received his family name from Edmund of Langley, Duke of York, Edward III's fourth son, but he claimed precedence over the house of Lancaster by right of his descent through the female line from Edward's second son, Lionel. Far more serious than genealogical niceties, however, was political and military reality. A disputed pedigree would have meant nothing to a monarch who ruled by right of two generations of kingship if he had been able to prove himself both in the council chamber and the bedroom. Unfortunately Henry VI was both incompetent and, until 1453, childless. York was undeniably next in line to the throne, a fact that was recognized in 1447. As heir apparent he sought to dominate the king's council, controlling the profits of royal government and manipulating the kindly but unkingly sovereign. The duke, however, did not depend upon blood alone to substantiate his claim to the crown or to control the council. He was the head of a powerful baronial galaxy, consisting of seventeen peers out of a titled aristocracy of about sixty, and the titular leader of a Yorkist system of lordships that reached into every shire of the kingdom.

A sketch of "the Kingmaker," the opportunistic Richard Neville, Earl of Warwick, who fought as Yorkist and Lancastrian, was made after his death in 1471.

The root of the matter was that almost anybody could influence Henry, who, as one observer remarked, had not "the heart or manliness to be a king" and was more concerned with his soul's health than with the sordid intrigues of politics. Unfortunately Richard of York and his gang were not the only ones attempting to breathe self-interested advice into the monarch's ear; at every turn they were blocked at court and on the council by a rival Lancastrian clique led by the king's Beaufort cousin Edmund, Duke of Somerset, in alliance with the queen, Margaret of Anjou. Henry VI was maneuvered by Somerset and Queen Margaret into becoming the head of a Lancastrian political party, and the results were disastrous to royal prestige. A Lancastrian sovereign could not expect his subjects to remain loyal when he was behaving in Norfolk exactly as the Duke of York had behaved in Lincolnshire. The Pastons of Norfolk were justifiably outraged in 1448 when Robert Hungerford, Lord Moleyns, with a hundred men ejected Mrs. Paston from her manor house of Gresham and then secured a letter from Henry VI instructing the sheriff to "make such a panell as to acquyte the Lord Moleynes." Henry had become a party chief, not a king.

Political bickering within the king's council around a man who was far too nice to be an effective ruler might never have exploded into armed revolt had not fate forced York's hand. In August of 1453, at the age of thirty-two, Henry VI suddenly and inexplicably fell into "so sudden and terrible . . . an infirmity that he had neither natural feeling nor sense of reason." To make matters worse, two months later Queen Margaret gave birth to a male child, Edward, Prince of Wales, thereby displacing the duke as heir to the throne. During the crisis following the onset of the king's insanity York was regent, but his authority lasted no longer than Henry's illness, which ended as unexpectedly as it had begun; in February of 1455 he recovered his senses and slyly announced to his startled court that his son must have been fathered by the Holy Ghost.

Exactly when the decision to use force was made is not known, but in an atmosphere of growing mistrust and mutual incrimination, each side began to take "precautionary" measures, quietly alerting members, arming retainers, and stocking arsenals. In the end the inevitable occurred; in May of 1455 two ridiculously small bands of soldiers met by accident in the streets of St. Albans, and the so-called Wars of the Roses began. St. Albans was in fact more murder than war. The number killed was scarcely sixty, and the fighting ceased the moment York's young nephew Richard Neville, Earl of Warwick, settled his score with the Earl of Northumberland and Lord Clifford, and when Duke Richard himself had seen to the slaying of his political rival the Duke of Somerset.

The assassination of Somerset won Richard of York momentary control of the king's council and Richard Neville supremacy over his enemies in the north, but both leaders earned the hatred of the remaining Lancastrian nobility, especially the queen, "a great and strong-labored woman" who succeeded in frustrating the duke's every move. Frantically both sides marshalled their forces and sought outside aid—York turning to Burgundy and

Margaret to Scotland and France. By the autumn of 1460 the situation had become intolerable: the realities and legalities of power had parted company. Henry was king in name, but he lacked the desire and ability to exercise his authority; York and Queen Margaret controlled the realities of military and political power but could not co-operate. No one quite knew where justice lay—with Duke Richard, who called himself the champion of good government but had to risk regicide to achieve it, or with Margaret and her greedy crew, who possessed two trump cards: the docile Henry VI and his young son, to whom a majority of the Lancastrian nobility remained hesitantly faithful.

The crisis came in October of 1460 when York made his first overt grab for the scepter. The scene at the opening of Parliament was tense and dramatic. The Duke of York "suddenly arrived, with great pomp and splendor, and in no little exaltation of spirit . . . entering the palace he went straight through the great hall until he came to the usual room, where the king, with the commons, was accustomed to hold his parliament. And coming there he walked straight on, until he came to the king's throne." Then he placed his hand upon the royal cushion, as if taking possession of what was his by right, and turned to face the Lords and Commons, eagerly looking for their applause. In an agony of uncertainty the duke stood under the canopy of state, daring neither to step down nor to seize the throne. At this moment Thomas Bourchier, Archbishop of Canterbury, called York's bluff. Rising up, he politely asked if his lordship "would come and see the king." The duke, "as if stung in soul by this question, replied shortly, 'I do not recall that I know anyone within the kingdom whom it would not befit to come sooner to me and see me rather than I should go and visit him.'"

The only crown Duke Richard was ever to wear was in death. On December 30, 1460, a small Yorkist force at

With the beheading of the fourth Duke of Somerset after the Yorkist triumph at the battle of Tewkesbury, the powerful Lancastrian Beauforts became extinct.

Wakefield was ambushed and annihilated; the duke was killed, and his battered brow was crowned with paper in derision of his claim to the throne. His younger son, the Earl of Rutland, was captured and murdered by Lord Clifford, whose father had fallen at St. Albans. When Rutland begged for his life, Clifford's answer was brief but barbaric: "By God's blood, thy father slew mine, and so will I do to thee and all thy kin." State it as you will—as a Shakespearean curse, or in sociopsychological terms—the habit of civilized behavior, of compassion and self-restraint, had vanished: "all pity choked with custom of fell deeds."

With York's death Clifford's creed of vengeance triumphed; where the father hesitated at seizing the throne, the eldest son—Edward, Duke of York—now claimed it as his birthright and swore revenge. Victory did not come easily, for the queen still possessed the body of the confused but legal king, and she was successful in rallying the Lancastrian cause around the person of her son. At the second battle of St. Albans, in February, 1461, she almost ended the Yorkist threat by badly beating the Earl of Warwick; but the battle of Mortimer's Cross, two weeks earlier, had been another story. Then young Edward of York himself was in charge, and the Lancastrian army had fled. St. Albans and Mortimer's Cross

were but dress rehearsals for the bloodiest battle of all, fought at Towton on Palm Sunday. No one paid any attention to the pious pleas of Henry VI that the armies meet in peace that day or to the tradition that whenever Englishmen fought Englishmen there should always first be an effort to settle the quarrel by discussion. Instead possibly ten thousand died in a nightmare when the flower of the Lancastrian nobility perished in the blinding snow and icy waters of Cork stream, a tiny brook swollen by the winter's rain.

After Towton one might have thought that the Lancastrian cup of misery was full, but God's wrath had still to be propitiated; vengeance required that yet another "king anointed, crowned and consecrate" be humiliated and destroyed. After the battle Henry VI and his queen escaped north to Scotland, while Edward IV rode south to his coronation at Westminster. For three miserable years the Lancastrian fortunes continued to wane. By the spring of 1463 Henry was a fugitive in his own kingdom, and a year later his hiding place was finally betrayed by a Black Monk of Abingdon. Henry rode from Lancashire to London with his legs tied to his stirrups, and when he arrived at the Tower, nobody even bothered with a formal abdication, "so amazed and utterly dulled with troubles and adversity" was the defrocked king.

Once Henry was safely incarcerated, Edward's greatest danger lay not with his Lancastrian enemies but with his Yorkist friends. His cousin Richard Neville, Earl of Warwick, had been largely responsible for winning Edward his crown, but the new royal master and his noble kingmaker soon fell out. By 1471 Warwick, in league with Queen Margaret, was up to his old tricks—this time seeking to reinstate Henry VI. Fortunately for Edward the kingdom was weary of a militant queen, an overmighty kingmaker, and a senile monarch, and the response was cool. At Barnet on the fourteenth of April, 1471, in a fog so

ELIZABETHA · VXOR
HENRICI · VII ·

The last Yorkist was Elizabeth, eldest daughter of Edward IV, who in 1486 married Henry VII—the last, and most dubious, Lancastrian. In this contemporary portrait she holds a Yorkist rose.

thick that the soldiers could not distinguish friend from foe and the dying "looked up for heaven and only saw the mist," Warwick was killed trying to escape. Three weeks later the final Lancastrian calamity took place at Tewkesbury; Queen Margaret was captured and the Prince of Wales killed, though he begged on his knees for his life. Then the chessboard was swept totally clean: on the twenty-first of May, in the Tower of London, Henry VI was quietly murdered.

The gods, alas, cannot be trusted. The very extent of the Lancastrian debacle eventually proved to be the Yorkist undoing. So much royal blood had been spilled during two generations of baronial war that the Lancastrian title passed to an obscure Welshman, Henry Tudor, Earl of Richmond, whose right to the throne was suspect twice over. His grandfather Owen Tudor, a clerk of the wardrobe, had successfully consoled the widowed queen of Henry V in her bereavement, and four children had resulted from his efforts. What is not established is whether their offspring were born before or after the wedding ceremony. On his mother's side Henry was a Beaufort, claiming descent from the illegitimate union of John of Gaunt, Duke of Lancaster, and his mistress Catherine Swynford. Gaunt eventually married Catherine, and their children were legitimized, although they were barred from the succession to the throne. By 1471, however, the Lancastrian line was so barren that even such a questionable pedigree was enough to make Henry Tudor the Lancastrian heir. As early as 1461 the potential Tudor threat had been recognized when Edward IV at the battle of Mortimer's Cross set the head of old Owen Tudor upon the highest step of the market cross, where a madwoman combed its hair and washed the sightless face. After the Lancastrian disaster at Tewkesbury the only safe place for Henry Tudor was in exile, where he remained for twenty-four long years.

Technically the Wars of the Roses ended in 1471; the tight cycle of armed revolt, governmental paralysis, and economic stagnation slowly gave way as commercial prosperity, financial solvency, and royal justice reasserted themselves. But from Shakespeare's perspective the conclusion could not be reached until "disorder, horror, fear and mutiny" had run their appointed course and the Tudor phoenix had risen from the ashes of dynastic war. The poet may be right; like Humpty Dumpty, society, once it had gone wrong, could not be reconstructed by all the king's horses or all the king's men. By the time of Edward IV's death in 1483 the Yorkist dynasty had still not been able to pick up the pieces or retie the strings of loyalty, and the king's twelve-year-old son fell victim to the usual forces of social disintegration. Such had become the habit of regicide that young Edward V reigned less than three months before his crown was usurped by his uncle Richard, Duke of Gloucester.

The evils of lordship and the spiral of economic contraction did not cease overnight when Henry Tudor returned from exile and took the gamble that Lancastrian luck had finally changed and that retribution had been made in full. Nor did violence and political anarchy come to an end on August 22, 1485, when Richard III fell and Henry Tudor, Earl of Richmond, triumphed at Bosworth Field. But the fragile shell of a new society built upon fresh ties of devotion and renewed willingness to sacrifice private gain for public good was uniquely the work of the great Tudor monarchs. Certainly Shakespeare and all his generation were quite sure that civil wounds were healed and peace lived once again only when Henry VII united the warring roses by marrying Elizabeth of York, the eldest daughter of Edward IV, and proclaimed:

We will unite the white rose and the red:
Smile, heaven, upon this fair conjunction,
That long have frown'd upon their enmity!
What traitor hears me, and says not amen?
England hath long been mad, and scarr'd herself;
The brother blindly shed the brother's blood,
The father rashly slaughter'd his own son,
The son, compell'd, been butcher to the sire:
All this divided York and Lancaster,
Divided in their dire division,
O! now, let Richmond and Elizabeth,
The true succeeders of each royal house,
By God's fair ordinance conjoin together;
And let their heirs—God, if thy will be so—
Enrich the time to come with smooth-fac'd peace,
With smiling plenty, and fair prosperous days!

Lacey Baldwin Smith, Professor of History at Northwestern University, is the author of The Horizon Book of the Elizabethan World. *His most recent essay for the magazine, "England's Second Family: the Cecils," appeared in the issue of Autumn, 1967.*

The first Tudor king, Henry VII, is depicted by an unknown artist of the time as a man of peace—holding a white and red rose, symbol of reunion between the factions. He took the throne after defeating Richard II at Bosworth Field in 1485.

AN ARTIST IN HIS STUDIO

Allegory or autobiography? No one can say with certainty. But Jan Vermeer doubtless knew, when he sat down to paint this serene masterpiece, that the universal is often most eloquently stated in the intensely personal

Judging from his painting *An Artist in His Studio,* it might be assumed that Jan Vermeer was quite a commercial success. For if the richly dressed artist with his back to us is indeed Vermeer, he shows himself at work in a bright, prosperous, even opulent, atmosphere that would probably gladden the soul of any artist forced to work indoors. The room, in the best Dutch tradition, is clean and refined looking; the floor tiles are well scrubbed, the brass chandelier buffed like a Pullman spittoon. A Turkish carpet swooping down from the ceiling looks like an idealization of prosperity and success.

Unfortunately, this happy painted image does not coincide with the facts of history, for Vermeer, as far as we know from the scant evidence, was one of those rare yet often cited cases of an artist who lived out his short life in perpetual debt without attaining any significant commercial success.

The personality of such a failure is usually a combination of social rebel and aesthetic revolutionary. Vermeer was neither. He quite easily adhered to the genres and traditions of his time, and his technique, though fraught with subtle innovations of color, shading, and a type of pointillism, was not such that it would in any way alienate him from the average seventeenth-century Dutch art lover. In fact, even in his subject matter Vermeer was a solid man of his time; the clean geometric interiors he favored are so like those of his contemporary Pieter de Hooch (except to the cultured eye) that the two were quite often mistaken in the nineteenth century.

Assuming that Vermeer painted according to the accepted standards of the time, was he, then, one of those impossible, self-conscious introverts who refused to show their work or pander to the fickle commercial tastes of the day? Not likely. At twenty-one Vermeer took the trouble to seek and gain admission to the painters' guild of Delft so that he might officially offer his work for sale. A recluse would hardly have bothered with a guild, nor would he have established such a neat, workable, and inviting atelier as that depicted in the *Artist in His Studio.*

Assumptions are enticing in the face of meager facts, and in the case of Vermeer art historians have understandably indulged themselves, seeking some sort of valid explanation for his unreasonable failure. It has been said, for example, that he could not sell his work in Protestant Holland because his wife was Catholic. Some have suggested that chronic illness kept him from producing a large number of paintings and deprived him of the energy necessary to sell those he did produce. But in 1671—four years before his death—Vermeer mustered enough energy to travel to The Hague to make a grueling evaluation of certain Italian paintings acquired by the Elector of Brandenburg.

It may be that Vermeer's failure was due to his own terribly personal image of success, his transcendent view of what an honest artist should be despite all intervening circumstances. In a phrase, he became—by an introspective, self-preserving choice—a kind of Sunday painter, a "great amateur," as Sir Kenneth Clark called him; not a dabbler or an incompetent, but an amateur in the highest sense of "one who loves." Both in his work and probably in his life, as Sir Kenneth says, "no other artist has had so fine a sense of withdrawal"—and no other artist made such a point of it. Jan Vermeer, so it seems from *An Artist in His Studio,* very carefully dressed up in his best clothes for the poignant purpose of quite openly glorifying and subsequently immortalizing his professional failure.

Vermeer was born in Delft in the autumn of 1632—the same year as Spinoza in Amsterdam and as his fellow townsman the microscopist Leeuwenhoeck—and in October was baptized Joannes (or Jan). His father was, among other things, an innkeeper and an art dealer, professions that Jan presumably also followed. In April, 1653, Vermeer married Catharina Bolnes, who bore him eleven children. In the year of his marriage he was received in the local artists' guild, the Guild of St. Luke, eventually serving twice as its president. This office does not seem to have been of much practical help to

By OWEN RACHLEFF

AN ARTIST IN HIS STUDIO, OIL ON CANVAS (51¼ x 43¼)

OVERLEAF: *A detail shows the artist and his model, a girl bearing trumpet and book, who is probably Vermeer's wife.*

him, for in all his days, up to his death in 1675 at the age of forty-three, Vermeer never recorded a single sale of one of his own paintings. The most we can say of them, commercially, is that several were deposited as collateral against purchases—with his baker, for example, for an enormous bread bill— and as payments for debts. *An Artist in His Studio* cleared a posthumous debt with his mother-in-law, and his widow was obliged to declare herself bankrupt in 1676.

As for fame, he had none. His official occupation was presumably art dealer, and his place of business the tavern left him by his father. This establishment, called "Mechelen," also served as Vermeer's home and studio (up to 1672) and was located on the busy market square in Delft. Combining an art gallery and a tavern was no rarity in those days, since the enterprising Dutch viewed paintings as they viewed any other salable product. As an English visitor to Holland in 1641, John Evelyn, wrote in his diary: ". . . their annual marte or faire [was] so furnished with pictures . . . that I was amaz'd . . . it is an ordinary thing to find a common farmer lay out two or 3,000 £ in this comodity. Their houses are full of them and they vend them at their faires to very great gains."

Well, not Vermeer. The pictures he vended in his tavern were painted by other artists. One can imagine this sensitive and quiet young man, even as an art dealer, withdrawing farther and farther from the hubbub of merchandising that "amaz'd" John Evelyn, until his business shriveled away. It was apparently a rough-and-tumble trade, and it took a thick skin to survive in it.

There were other factors that surely were unsettling to Vermeer, especially toward the end of his life. The French

Vermeer bestowed a vivid reality on even the smallest details of his paintings. Opposite, the chandelier in An Artist in His Studio *richly reflects the myriad variations of light. The bay in the upper corner of the map is the Zuider Zee.*

This detail from Vermeer's The Procuress *is probably the artist's self-portrait. He wears the same shirt and hat as the painter in* An Artist in His Studio.

invasion in 1672, the subsequent falling off of prosperity in Holland—externals like these can often help to capsize an introspective man. And so, perhaps, he sighed and retired to the easel, not just to paint a picture, but to paint a dream.

The canvas he painted in this frame of mind was large (51¼" x 43¼"). Some say it was painted around 1666. It may well have been done later however, sometime after 1672; for the setting of this painting—the studio—appears to be a dining room in Vermeer's small house on the Oude Langendijk, to which he moved in May, 1672, after vacating Mechelen. Max Eisler, who wrote about Vermeer in the 1900's, believes that *Studio* was probably the last thing Vermeer worked on, and Eisler is very likely correct; the painting was, after all, still in Vermeer's studio after his death and was used to clear a posthumous debt. Many of his earlier works had long since been impounded by various tradesmen and creditors.

The setting shown in the painting also came to light after Vermeer's death. At the time, an inventory was made of his personal art collection. According to this document, the art historian Ludwig Goldscheider points out, the painting called *Christ on the Cross*, by Jordaens—the very painting Vermeer depicted in *Allegory of the New Testament*—was the one listed as hanging in Vermeer's dining room. Owing to the similarity between the

ceiling beams in *New Testament* (see page 101) and *Studio*, we can, somewhat extravagantly, extend Goldscheider's diningroom theory to include *Studio* also. How well this fits in with our image of the Sunday painter creating sweet classical dreams while the odors of stew and pudding linger in the air!

Another assumption that is often made is that the painting is actually a conscious allegory, in fact an allegory of art, in which a painter is portrayed in the sacred act of immortalizing Fame, or History, who, as a Muse, has literally descended into his studio. Yet, more than an allegory, it is a naturalistic painting—quiet, warm, autobiographical. Even the time of year and the time of day can be deduced. The season, for example, appears to be spring or summer—at least the weather is warm—for there are no candles in the chandelier, lest they warp in the sunlight. And it is probably morning: Vermeer has just begun work on his canvas, painting in the laurel crown of the model while the rest of the figure remains outlined in chalk.

We can also gather from the painting some idea of the everyday manner in which the artist worked. Holding a palette (not visible) in his left hand, along with a mahlstick to steady his right, Vermeer—if it be he—has begun by laying in a prime coat of gray on the canvas and an undercoat of blue and gray for the laurel crown. It should be noted here that something may have happened to the color of the actual laurel leaves on the model's head. André Malraux believes that they were once green and that a change, a subtle fading of the yellow elements, must have taken place. Yet Vermeer may have purposely intended them to be blue, not green; we know how much he favored basic blues, grays, and pearly whites over the more conventional warmer tones. As a result of this preference Vermeer's work always has a cool, bluish cast that most realistically approximates natural daylight. This uncanny coolness of color, which

Recurrent Motifs

The same room with variations framed Vermeer's artistic world even in his least typical work, Allegory of the New Testament, *opposite. The room had a checkerboard floor, beam ceiling, and a window on the left as you enter. Only in Vermeer's* Lacemaker, *opposite, does light come from the right. The map and the heavy drapery of* An Artist in His Studio *can be seen again and again in Vermeer's household cosmos, along with its presiding deity, a sweet-faced woman with a high, round forehead, his wife.*

WOMAN IN BLUE READING A LETTER

LADY READING A LETTER AT AN OPEN WINDOW

is evident even in the artist's use of traditionally warm tones, such as yellow, was keenly appreciated by the nineteenth-century Vermeer specialist E. J. T. Thoré-Bürger, who said: "[He] captured silver in his light and pearls in his shadows . . . [and though] as in nature the colors are antipathetic —for example yellow and blue—they are not at all discordant." Van Gogh was also struck by the "lemon yellow, dull blue, and light gray" characteristic of Vermeer. Only comparisons with other Dutch masters of the time— Rembrandt, Hals, Terborch, De Hooch—can reveal the personal intensity of this strange fluorescent light.

The figures in this "dream" painting bear out a certain wish-fulfillment idea. Of course, there has been some doubt about who the figures are; a nineteenth-century description of the canvas indicated that the artist represented was in fact Pieter de Hooch. No one accepts that now. However art historians do say that it may not be Vermeer, but rather his symbolic representation of man-as-an-artist; and because Vermeer self-portraits are rare, they think they need not argue further. But Vermeer would probably not have been so calculating as to exclude himself from the focus of his dream, and though he averts his face from the viewer, in the interests of composition, he manages subtly to tell us who the artist is by relating his appearance to a work called *The Procuress,* of 1656 —one of the few works we can accu-

rately date—in which we find what has long reasonably been presumed to be Vermeer's only frontal self-portrait. In it he wears the same ribboned shirt and the same cap that he wears in *Studio,* although the lacy collar has disappeared in the fifteen- or sixteen-year interval between paintings. His distinctive fluffy hairdo is also identical in both.

The artist's model has been even more baffling to viewers. It is she, in fact, who has provoked the "allegory" idea, mainly because she has assumed a classic costume and pose. Some say that she is Clio, the Muse of history (note her trumpet and tome). Others call her Fame, the "trumpeter" of glory. The plaster mask lying near her on the table, along with a book, a scroll, and some swaths of silk, supposedly enhances the classical aura. But casual perusal of the model's face makes us realize after all that she is a very real and ordinary person, not a goddess. Furthermore, those familiar with Vermeer's women will see at once that she seems to be the same person who appears in many of his other works— Catharina, his wife. True, he has set a crown of laurels on her head and wrapped her in blue satin; true, he has decorated the scene with classical symbols. But a wreath alone does not a goddess make, and such symbols as he used could be found in many an artist's trunk. Besides, how much more human the picture becomes when we think that our great Sunday painter has once

again prevailed upon his soft-mouthed wife to pose for him and this time has dressed her up as a muse or goddess. Certainly Vermeer had neither the money nor the need to hire a professional model, and in his mind the repetition of this face (which first appears in *The Procuress*), like the repetition of floors, tapestries, maps, binds his work together.

Another repeated element found in Vermeer's work is the reversed figure, the one with his back toward the audience, so to speak. In *Studio* Vermeer no doubt resorted to a trick of optics in order to achieve this rear view of himself. Two or three mirrors were probably set up in front of the easel and two or three behind, so that the artist could catch the image of his own back. (This reversed image of Vermeer, by the way, was duplicated by Salvador Dali in his *Ghost of Vermeer* and the *Enigmatic Landscape.*)

Conceptually, the reverse figure is the result of a rather sophisticated desire on the artist's part never to draw attention away from his central figure. Vermeer knew the old truth about the immediate attraction of the human face, especially the eyes. Nevertheless, he softens this impact in *Studio* by directing the model's eyes downward toward the table. The result is a more general focus. We are not drawn directly to the lady, but first to the bright white shirt of the artist, then to the yellow book that the model holds, and in succession to her face, her

THE LACEMAKER

THE CONCERT

ALLEGORY OF THE NEW TESTAMENT

trumpet, and the daylight glow that surrounds her at the left. In Vermeer's tight, subtle world of painting, the light almost invariably flows from the left; the famous portrait of the *Lacemaker*, now in the Louvre (see above), is one of the few exceptions. The left side of the canvas is also his favorite location for drapery, which serves in the baroque tradition as an inner frame for the central idea. Vermeer's drape in *Studio*, as in most of his later works, is actually a carpet, here suspended from the ceiling beams and held in a graceful fold by the chair at left.

One other leitmotif is worth noting: the map. The Dutch of the mid-seventeenth century were very conscious of their hard-won nationality and of their expanding colonial empire. Maps were eagerly sought and prolifically reproduced. This one is a fairly elaborate creation by a cartographer signing himself Nicolaum Piscatorem (his name can be made out on the dark border behind the chandelier). It shows the Netherlands in Habsburg days, its chief cities and sites categorized within oval margin illustrations reminiscent of the decorations found on delftware even to this day. In Vermeer's hands this map is a rare artistic achievement, for it should be pointed out that rendering two-dimensional outlines in a painting, such as lettering and decorations, is an art in itself and when not successfully done, an awkward stumbling block.

Writing of *An Artist in His Studio*, the American critic James G. Huneker was unequivocal. "It is a masterpiece," he said; "in it [Vermeer] grazes perfection." The verb is apt, for subtlety is ever Vermeer's art. Pre-eminently in his time, he mastered the ability to sweep the freshness and light of *plein air* into the cubicles of the Dutch interior. Daintily, as one viewer put it, he immerged everyday objects into unseen spatial prisms that not only break up and reflect the illusive light but above all imprison it in places, as though the canvas had been transubstantiated into a fluorescent tube. We are moved to touch it, if we dare, to see if there is actual space between the objects and heat in the seductive, glowing areas.

We are amazed to find an everyday interior uplifted into a beautiful and rarified space, a space in which we have been living, without realizing its beauty, for so long. Vermeer, by his genius, has done for man's ordinary rooms what the Italian painters of the Renaissance did for man's ordinary bodies. In the midst of domesticity, surrounded by chairs, tables, bric-a-brac, and drapery, we seem to be nonetheless in a special kind of wonderland.

Yet for all our modern excitement and praise, the painting remained in oblivion for nearly two hundred years after Vermeer's death. First, as we have seen, it served to pay a family debt. Then it appears to have shown up in 1696 at an auction in Amsterdam and been sold, cheaply, to a Viennese collector. In 1813 a certain Count Czernin grabbed it up for fifty Austrian guilders, believing it to be a painting by De Hooch. Not until 1860 was it recognized as a Vermeer. By then, owing to Thoré-Bürger, the artist from Delft had become a celebrity and the Czernin family proudly held onto its prize; until 1942, that is, when this lovely and serene work of art was transferred to the private chambers of Adolf Hitler at Berchtesgaden. Liberated by the Allies in 1945, it was installed in Vienna's Kunsthistorisches Museum, where it now resides.

Wilhelm von Bode, the specialist in Dutch art, has remarked: "Holland has indeed shown little generosity to her artists who have been principally the means of making the glory of their country known to posterity." We think of Rembrandt, Hals, Hobbema, and others suffering from seventeenth-century public indifference, and we know that Bode is right. Accepting this situation as a fact of life, Vermeer was left with the sole comfort of his art. But was that really enough in the face of debts and doubts? Did it ease the tragedy of an early death?

Hardly. For artists need laurels just as do the gods. Vermeer, despite his "amateur status," seems to be saying this as he begins to paint the laurel crown before our very eyes.

Owen Rachleff is a playwright and art historian; he lectures on art at the New School and at New York University.

Vermeer's Delft

As far as we know, Jan Vermeer, as a painter, only stepped twice beyond the confines of his own house: once to paint a little street scene, the other time to do what is very likely the greatest townscape ever painted—his *View of Delft,* shown at right. In this masterpiece of tranquillity and clear, clean light, Vermeer paid his homage to the quiet, genteel city in which he himself lived so quietly. It was, characteristically, a realistic homage, for the stately repose of the painting was the prevailing spirit of Vermeer's Delft, a town that seemed to have abjured coarseness even in making its livelihood. Fine tapestries, fine earthenware, deep carpets, and optical instruments were the handiwork of Delft's artisans. A Chamber of Rhetoric, where citizens could partake of the beauties of art, was one of its municipal features, and men of sturdy self-cultivation were another. It is no accident that one of the greatest self-taught discoverers in science, the microscopist Anton van Leeuwenhoek, was a Delft man, and that one of the world's supreme artists, Vermeer himself, had no known instructor.

In this and other ways Vermeer was a true Delft man: he shared the city's love of meticulous workmanship, its fondness for realism, and its profound domesticity. Little though Delft paid him notice, it did not, by all accounts, discontent him, for he lived there all his life and left it perhaps only once. Few men of genius are so fixed in place, and an apt emblem of that fixity can be found in Vermeer's townscape itself. The steeple at the right belongs to Delft's New Church, where Vermeer was baptized; the steeple on the left marks the Old Church, where he was buried. In between lay a few hundred yards and forty-three years of life for a very private man who transmuted the privacy of the home into the highest art.

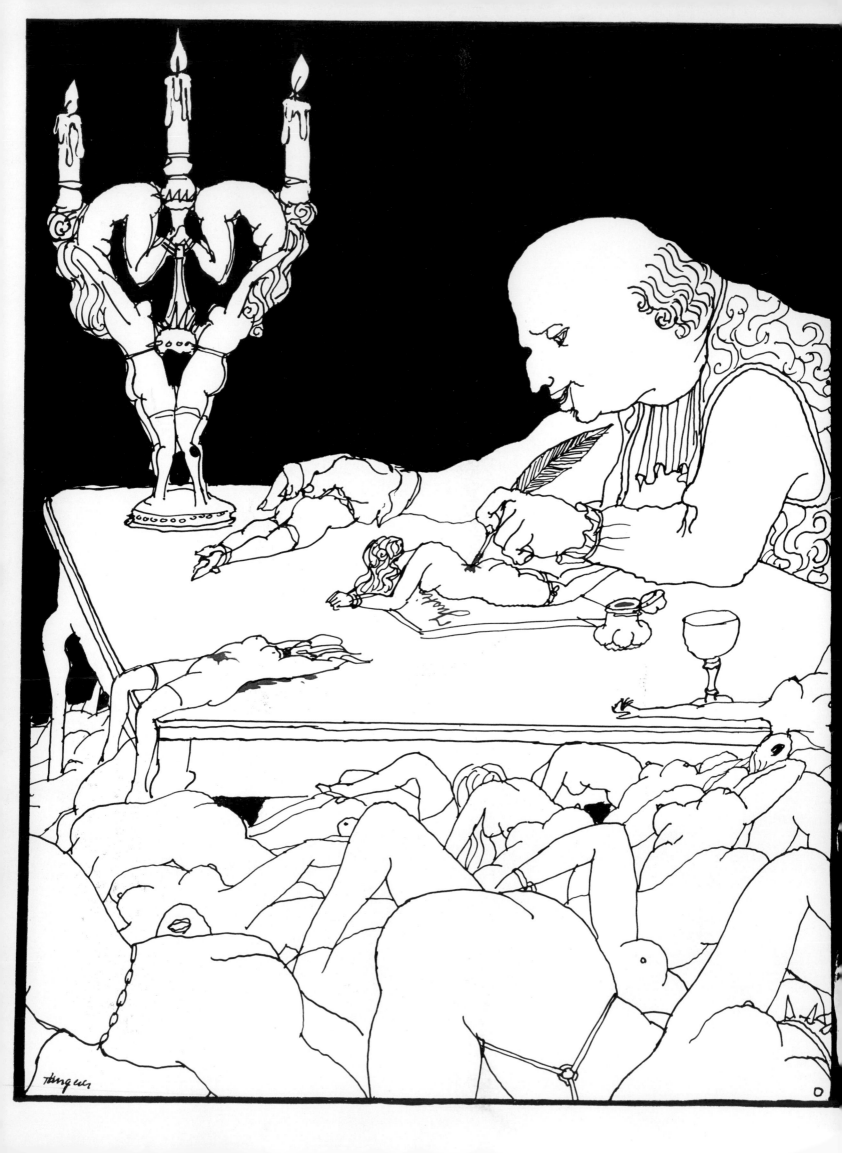

OUR BEDFELLOW

THE MARQUIS DE SADE

With his whips and knives and dreams of mass destruction, "he knew what we have taken a long time to learn—that sex is not just something that happens in a bedroom"

Only two writers in the whole of world literature have, solely on the strength of the philosophies they preached, been elevated into monstrous figures of evil. The first was Niccolò Machiavelli, whose book on statecraft, *Il Principe* (*The Prince*), was not well understood by his chief traducers, the Elizabethan English. The popular view of "Old Nick" (yes, that's where the diabolic sobriquet comes from) was of a bogeyman dedicated to the subversion of good, the liquidation of religion, and the promotion of death and violence for their own sake. A close reading of *Il Principe* shows that Machiavelli went, in fact, nowhere near so far: he was concerned with a very laudable end—that of maintaining order in a community threatened by enemies without and traitors within. What earned him such extravagant odium was his lack of scruple about the means by which that end should be fulfilled. Every state, even the most liberal and democratic, has in time of emergency had to use Machiavellian devices; yet mention the term, or preferably whisper it ("*Machiavellian!*"), and the response is a shuddering one. The word has been loaded for centuries.

The second of these writers is the Marquis de Sade, and till recently, the term sadism has not carried the full load of horror available to it. The most

popular joke that admits the perversion and its complement is about the sadist and the masochist who share adjoining beds in a psychiatric ward. "Beat me, beat me!" cries the masochist. "No," says the sadist. But that is not it at all: there is nothing negative in sadism. And the small torturer, the boy who pulls wings off flies, the husband who drops burning brown paper on his wife's bare body—these don't go far enough. The extravagance of evil falsely attributed to Machiavelli should, by rights, be transferred to the Marquis. But few people have read his works, and few imaginations are capable of reaching the ingenuities of his fancies. It is only fairly recently that this devil has been given his due.

Pamela Hansford Johnson, the novelist, has published a book called *On Iniquity*, which consists chiefly of moral meditations on the hideous "Moors Murders" in England. These, as everyone knows by now, were perpetrated for no end of gain or revenge. They were disinterested and very sophisticated acts of horror in which dying screams were taped and edited with a mélange of popular music, in which the tortures administered were "beyond belief," and for which there was no expression of remorse.

The murderers were discovered to

possess, along with *Mein Kampf* and various cheap examples of the pornography of violence, a copy of *Justine*, one of the few works of the Marquis de Sade available to the British public. Miss Johnson raises, albeit with diffidence, the question of the desirability of suppressing any book that leads to even one sadistic murder, and the question is still being earnestly debated. If a work of the Marquis de Sade is capable of inspiring acts of lethal cruelty, should not his name be thrust back again into the darkness?

I don't think so. I think it is very important that the Marquis be brought into the bright light of close examination. He is one of the prophets of our age. As for his malign influence—well, it has already been pretty conclusively demonstrated that when there is a will to cruelty and murder, the pretext of a literary example is supererogatory. Besides, we would have to rid the world of some of its noblest, even holiest, books if we wanted to prevent literature from abetting evil. Leon Friedman, a New York lawyer, replying to Miss Johnson in a letter to *Encounter* magazine, points out that Albert Fish, "who killed at least five young children and tortured or sexually abused perhaps hundreds of others," gained his inspiration from the Bible—Abraham's sacrifice of Isaac as an expia-

By ANTHONY BURGESS

tion of sin. We do not have to recoil from the Marquis de Sade any more than we have to from Nietzsche (whom the Nazis claimed as the patron of their Jew-killing) or from Shakespeare (whose *Hamlet* might have taught many an impressionable young man to kill his stepfather). We have to keep cool and study our author with no flicker of the pulse or mounting of blood to the head.

The De Sades were an old Provençal family, noble as far back as the twelfth century. One of their few literary claims to notice—they achieved eminence mostly in the church and the army—was the fact that the Laura of Petrarch's sonnets was a certain Laure de Sade, ironical when one considers what their most famous and infamous scion was to make out of the spiritual raptures of courtly love. He, Donatien Alphonse François de Sade, was born in Paris in 1740, the only son of a diplomat (his two sisters did not survive childhood). He was not allowed to accompany his father and mother when they went away on missions, and he was usually sent to stay with his grandmother. It has been Freudianly suggested that his mature taste for cruelty to women derived from his childish resentment of this maternal abandonment. But his grandmother made up for that neglect by spoiling him outrageously, feeding his youthful vanity and arrogance on tales of high connections on both sides of the family. At the age of five, he went to spend five years under the tutelage of his uncle, a learned but rather debauched *abbé*. After a more regular education from the Jesuits, he was taught to be a cavalry officer and, in the Seven Years' War of 1756–1763, distinguished himself as a captain full of fire and impetuosity. As a discharged soldier, he conscientiously got down to a life of gambling, debauchery, and general hell-raising in Paris. His father, who was a stiff man of the old school, was shocked and troubled: Donatien must be found a wife, made to settle down,

forcibly cooled and curbed.

And so, at the age of twenty-three, he married a certain Mlle. de Montreuil, by whom he was to have three children and, he hoped, a large inheritance from her father, the president of the board that worked out the taxes on wine and salt. But five months after the wedding Sade was arrested for certain unspecified acts of debauchery involving prostitutes and sent to prison in Vincennes for fifteen days. Released and back in Paris, he was honored by the special appointment of a police inspector, Monsieur Marais, to watch and pursue him. His life from now on was to be a matter of arrest, trial, and imprisonment. But his talent for debauchery of the most depraved and ingenious kind was totally irrepressible.

There was the case of Sade and Rose Keller, whom he forced to undress, flogged with a knotted whip, and then, according to Mlle. Keller, partially flayed with a pocketknife, pouring hot wax on the wounds. Sade did six months in a jail for that and would have done longer had not his uncle the *abbé* intervened, pleading that young Donatien's crime was no more than "giddiness and indiscretion." So the unexpired portion of the sentence was commuted to a moderate fine, and Sade was free to go to Marseilles, where there was a complicated orgy involving his valet, four prostitutes, sodomy, a whip with nails stuck in it, and some allegedly poisonous lozenges (Spanish fly?). This time, sodomy being a capital offense, Sade was condemned to death; but he escaped. The sentence was carried out only in effigy.

To sophisticate the growing body of scandal, Sade fell in love with his sister-in-law, who followed him to Italy after the Marseilles episode. It is evident that Sade was able to fascinate women, perhaps even to inspire genuine love; the devotion of his wife was slow to flag through all these horrible vicissitudes. After his escape from the fortress where the king of Sardinia had put him, he was back with her in his Provençal château, and she was apparently

concerned with protecting him, as far as she could, from the consequences of the most brutal escapades, most of them involving very young girls brought to the château as servants. Some of these sessions skated so close to murder that they begot a local belief that there was a special cemetery on the premises for the victims of Sade's peculiar tastes. He always denied that he was a murderer, but there was no getting over his local Jack-the-Ripper reputation. The women in the streets screamed when they saw him, and there were cries of "Werewolf"; nor was it easy to laugh off as someone's practical joke the presence of human bones in his garden.

Sade was certainly kept on the run from justice—off to Italy again, back to Provence, and eventually back to Paris, where (probably at the instance of his mother-in-law, who had obtained the legal instrument called a *lettre de cachet*) Inspector Marais caught him and had him committed to the prison at Vincennes. He was kept there, on and off, for seven years. Then, for another five, he was transferred to the Bastille. He left there just before that ancient symbol of oppression was stormed in 1789.

It would be satisfyingly ironic to think of this apostle of cruelty obtaining his release on July 14, along with the wronged innocents of *A Tale of Two Cities*, but only a few days before, he had been transferred to the lunatic asylum at Charenton. This was in consequence of furious allegations, shouted from his cell window to passers-by, that the Bastille governor was having the prisoners' throats slit (rather worse was done to the governor as soon as the Revolution started: his head was cut off and carried around on a pike). Sade stayed in the asylum for nine months, and then—sick, fat through lack of exercise, penniless, at last deserted by his wife—he lived wretchedly and misanthropically alone. But not for too long; a young actress, Marie-Constance Quesnet, attached herself to him, and their relationship seems to have been reasonably happy.

No longer a marquis, Sade became an "active citizen," a playwright and author of political pamphlets, an ardent sympathizer with the new movement (he had, after all, suffered in the Bastille). He rose to political office and even served as a judge, though he was violently against capital punishment (he had, after all, narrowly escaped it himself). Generally speaking, he was too unorthodox, too skeptical, to last long as a trusted officer of the Revolution. His enemies could still call him an *aristo*. By the end of 1793 he was back in prison again, and eventually his name was placed on a list of traitors to the Republic. The guillotine awaited him. But Robespierre fell the day after the first batch of victims on the list was executed, and with the start of a slightly more liberal phase in this bloody history, Sade was cleared, even lauded as a patriot. His luck could not last, however. He had already begun to publish the works of pornography that we must consider in a moment, and as a corruptive and dangerous character, he was yet again put safely away in jail, for two years in the prison of Sainte-Pélagie. In a notebook he wrote, "The entr'actes of my life have been too long."

After being removed, for an act of violence against other prisoners, to another jail, this time at Bicêtre, his family had him committed for the rest of his life to a place he already knew well—the madhouse at Charenton. The medical superintendent knew he was not really insane: "his only madness is that of vice," he said; but he failed to have him discharged and returned to prison. Sade's days were spent in free social intercourse and (as readers who have seen the *Marat/Sade* play will not need to be reminded) in the presentation of dramatic entertainments that the director of the asylum held to have a high therapeutic value for the genuinely deranged. Sade tried often enough to have himself removed—he even appealed to Napoleon, by then emperor; but Napoleon thought it best to leave him where he was. And so, sweetened

by the presence of Marie-Constance, who lived in the asylum with him, his days passed in the practice of a kind of art—an unrepentant dream, hardly broken, of pornographical violence—and he died in 1814.

It was in the prison at Vincennes, while he was serving his first long sentence and was cut off from the enactment of sexual cruelty, that Sade became a writer. He was anxious to shine primarily as a dramatist, but (this comes out all too strongly in his fiction) he lacked any real interest in moral conflict and resolution, and he had no gift for characterization. He really had only one theme—his own predilections and their justification through a rational philosophy. In his fifth year of imprisonment he produced a highly philosophical *Dialogue between a Priest and a Dying Man*. The priest calls for repentance, but meets only a powerful argument in favor of impenitence. "God," says the dying man, "made me what I am—corrupt and bent only on my own enjoyment (and, if you want repentance, all I repent is that I didn't find opportunities to enjoy myself even more than I did). It's no good your talking of free will, the ability to choose the good rather than the bad: God made both abilities, and evil seems to be as necessary to life as does its opposite. If God knew how my life would work out—in a guiltless preoccupation with pleasure—then God must be said to have willed it. Therefore what is there to repent? Besides, time is too short for argument, and there are six beautiful women waiting in the next room. Enjoy them with me; take pleasure in this life, which is sure though short: you can't give me any proof of another, better, life." This, anyway, is the gist. The priest succumbs, having no answer, and becomes as gladly corrupt as his interlocutor.

Though this dialogue mentions God a good deal, God was a concept that Sade wholly rejected (he was a good eighteenth-century rationalist in this). There is no God, but there is a goddess,

and this is Nature. We are wholly subject to her, being part of her, and we must fulfill in our own actions her most terrible and monstrous impulses. Nature is creative—lavishly and carelessly so, but she is also destructive, reveling in earthquakes, in storms, floods, volcanic eruptions. But this destructive urge is in the service of creating new forms of life. A huge melting pot is always on the boil, and her old creations are thrown into it, to re-emerge transmogrified. The devices of cruelty that man develops are a manifestation of quite impersonal, or rather prepersonal, energy. Personal guilt is irrelevant, since the first law of life is to accept the world as it is.

Sade's view of humanity is clearly at the opposite pole to that of his senior contemporary Jean Jacques Rousseau. Rousseau believed that the state of nature was all virtue and that man became depraved only through manmade laws (there is a contradiction in this philosophy). The Christian compromise doctrine—that man started out good but, through the wrong employment of the gift of free will, fell into a state of sin that is ultimately redemptible—is just as alien to Sade's convictions as the Romantic Rousseauan dream of a humanity that is rational and noble. The Sade image of man is, unfortunately, far more realistic than that of either Rousseau or the Church. In the depraved France of the prerevolutionary era, in the ghastly actions of the Terror, Sade could see ample evidence that man's appetites for pleasure were most satisfyingly fulfilled through the exercise of power and cruelty. His own private orgies, the extravagant fantasies of his books—what were these but reduced reflections of the conduct of the great world outside the château?

The world that George Orwell presents in *Nineteen Eighty-Four* owes a great deal to Sade. The ruling oligarchy knows what it is doing: it wants power, and it intends, behind the immortal, because mythical, façade of Big Brother, to keep power till the end of time. This power is the ultimate pleasure, the final human fulfillment. Its image is of a jackboot poised voluptuously over a terrified human face. The exercise of power means the exercise of cruelty, for it is only through cruelty that you can show your victim the extent of your total domination over him.

Sade's actions and, more patently, Sade's literary fantasies represented power as an aspect of the sexual impulse. The sexual act is shown not as a reciprocity of pleasure giving, but as the enforcing of strange desires on an unwilling victim. To share pleasure, said Sade, is to weaken it. The victim (like Winston Smith in *Nineteen Eighty-Four*) must be impotent to strike back and must be of a preordained persecutable type. In the sexual field it is women who are made for persecution: physiologically they are natural victims. Sade's major work, the unfinished *120 Days of Sodom*, is a detailed catalogue of sexual perversions, all of which involve torture and some of them death. The form of the book is fictional. The setting is a castle in the Black Forest, totally impregnable, and in it four debauchees from Paris—a banker, a bishop, a duke, and a judge —spend seventeen weeks in perverse pleasures that are graduated from the merely revolting to the ineffably and transcendently evil. It was Sade's intention to describe six hundred perversions, but he only managed to get through the first thirty days—though he made very detailed notes for the other ninety. Thus the seventy-ninth perversion in the "Third Class of Criminal Passions" entails strapping a naked girl face down to a table and having "a piping hot omelette served upon her buttocks." The eater "uses an exceedingly sharp fork." This is comparatively mild. The ultimate horror has fifteen girls (none older than seventeen) all tortured simultaneously in fifteen different ways, while the *grand seigneur* who arranges this elaborate *grand guignol* watches and waits for orgasm. It does not come easily, despite the monstrous stimulus: it has

to be effected through masturbation and the exhibition of two male bottoms.

It is evident that Sade, in conceiving these nightmares (nightmares to us; delicious dreams to him), was in a state of sexual frustration so intense that it drove him to a kind of clearheaded mania. The deprivations of prison life were an obvious factor, but they must be only a small part of the story. For Sade's dreams are essentially dreams of impotence, just as the recorded orgies on which some of the dreams are based are attempts to find satisfaction when the normal means have failed. The situation is not all that unusual. Eighteenth-century France was notable for its lecherous aristocracy, and Sade's youthful roistering was not more spectacular than that of many of his peers and superiors. But the normal sexual vein was overworked; the palate demanded sharper sauces. Or put it another way: the familiar intoxication could only, as with drug takers, be attained by stimulants that grew stronger and stronger.

The first stimulant was sodomy— one that has never been as rare as the law, which represses it mercilessly, would have us believe. Heterosexual sodomy (read the *Kama Sutra* on this) is a regular age-old practice among Tamils, and it carries little flavor of the perverse. But sodomy is selfish, and it can also be cruel. Sade was fascinated by it, and he is led through it to a genuinely nauseating preoccupation with the anus: he plays with feces like an infant.

When what may be termed pure sodomy fails to bring satisfaction, the next stage of cruelty is reached: the imposition of pain unconnected with coition and not necessarily centered on the erogenous zones. To inflict suffering is enough, by whatever means. But the more elementary forms—burning the flesh, cutting, flaying, even poisoning—must pall sooner or later, and then the sadist is led on to the more ingenious tortures, most of them slowly lethal. Where is the limit? The limit is

reached, it would seem, when heterosexual fantasies are swallowed up in apocalyptic visions of mass destruction —Hitlerian visions whose sexual content is not immediately apparent. Sade's destructive fantasies are curiously modern—the blasting of whole towns, a sort of *fête* in which "children are blown up by rockets and bombs." Edmund Wilson, to whose long essay on the Sade documents I am deeply indebted, says apropos of this: "How gratified Sade would have been if he could have foreseen the scale on which we were later to indulge in this pastime! Or would he perhaps have been appalled, as he was by the Terror?"

Sade was capable of being appalled; his sadism was not so thoroughgoing as, for total philosophical consistency, it ought to have been. But once you divide the world into victims and persecutors, you are faced with the problem of a frontier where roles may change: sadism tends to embrace its opposite, masochism. Leopold von Sacher-Masoch was born twenty-two years after Sade's death, but his stories about the pleasure of being hurt, degraded, dominated, are to some extent anticipated in the older master. While in prison at Vincennes, Sade regularly flagellated himself. The girls involved in the Marseilles orgy testified that the inflictions of cruelty were not all one-sided. Nowadays, informed by the sexologists of whom Sade was the true forerunner, we recognize in ourselves the dichotomy of our response to one of these magazine photographs we're always seeing—a girl in top boots with a whip or gun. "Kinky," we say, and shudder with two kinds of anticipatory pleasure: we identify with the torturer; we see ourselves as the victim.

That the sadomasochistic impulse is in all of us we no longer doubt. There is some obscure neural liaison in the brain between the sexual urge and the desire for domination—and the latter phrase I have deliberately left ambiguous. We are, quite rightly, scared of letting the sadomasochistic get out of hand: it is all too easy. We're all pretty bad inside; it's what we do outside that counts.

Sade, in his actions, and even more in his books, extrapolated on a Wagnerian scale what society insists on keeping locked in the crypts of the mind. Though vicious and perhaps demented, he does not belong to a race very different from our own. That is why he fascinates. But the fascination does not long survive the actual opening of one of his books. Nauseated by his anal fixations, we soon become bored with his ingenuities. Nobody is real; he seems to be playing with automata. He was interested in the art of the novel, and he wanted to contribute to the pornographic branch of it (in this he was merely one among many); but he was not sufficiently interested in people as people. There is no give and take, none of the dialectic of character that we find in competent fiction; there is only the wearying but unwearied catalogue of atrocities. The people who publish extracts from Sade in paperback are misrepresenting him: they are picking out the plums and putting in the wastebasket the dollops of farinaceous inedibility. Sade has to be given us entire, so that we may yawn over the long pages of eighteenth-century moralizing and become irritated by the self-contradictions. The public ought not to be titillated by half-censorship: the works of the Marquis de Sade ought to be freely available, and that would cure the smut hounds.

Has he any value in the history of literature or philosophy? His literary interest is slight though not entirely negligible. His philosophy of Nature is untenable but stimulating. Where he has to be taken seriously is in his role as pioneer sexologist. He was the first modern Western man to list the varieties of erotic perversion, and the list is pretty well exhaustive. Moreover, his view of sex is not limited to the European ethos. He was something of an anthropologist and argued that there was not one sexual practice regarded as perverse by the West that was not accepted as normal in some remoter

society. Most important of all, he saw with terrible clarity the sexual springs of cruelty, no matter how cruelly was disguised as a device of politics or of ecclesiastical discipline. Even in his recognition of the sexual elements that lie below family relationships and manifest themselves long before the age of puberty, he anticipated the Viennese school of psychology. He knew what we have taken a long time to learn—that sex is not just something that happens in a bedroom.

His profound misanthropy, while justified by the events of European history through which he lived, was not in conformity with the optimistic philosophies of his time. The chains of man could be broken, said Rousseau; reason could triumph, said the Encyclopedists. Sade never expected anything but the worst from mankind, so he could never be disappointed. He did not overestimate the rational capacities of man; however—following the custom of the age—he did invoke reason in his writings. Nowadays there are millions of people who find cause, far better cause than Sade had, to despair of the human race. Sade merely *dreamed* of chemists who could blow up whole cities; we have seen the reality of conventional high explosives and the thermonuclear bomb. His visions, like those of science fiction in our own day, were ahead of their time.

It is sourly amusing to observe where his true influence lies. The great dictators, bemused by dreams of national glory, have found him abhorrent (Napoleon was the first to be shocked). Schoolmasters with canes and parents with flat, hard hands have scarcely thought about him. It is the popular writers who have diluted his message and made it palatable to suburban minds. Ian Fleming, for instance:

"...I can tell you that the entire population of Fort Knox will be dead or incapacitated by midnight.... The substance that will be inserted in the water supply, outside the filter plant, will be a highly concentrated form of GB."

"You're mad! You don't really mean you're going to kill sixty thousand people!"

"Why not? American motorists do it every two years."

Bond stared into Goldfinger's face in fascinated horror. It couldn't be true! He couldn't mean it! He said tersely, "What's this GB?"

"GB is the most powerful of the Trilone group of nerve poisons. It was perfected by the Wehrmacht in 1943, but never used for fear of reprisals. In fact, it is a more effective instrument of destruction than the hydrogen bomb.... Introduction through the water supply is an ideal method of applying it to a densely populated area."

How the Marquis de Sade would have reveled in the technological triumphs that now, in literature, merely serve the end of a popular *frisson*.

In literature less popular, the misanthropy of Sade has become totally acceptable. I'm thinking particularly of William Golding's novel *The Inheritors*, where Homo sapiens, supervening on the gentle Neanderthals, destroys a worthier race because it is in his nature to destroy. Evil, Golding seems to say, is built into man. What do we do about that: acquiesce in it, as Sade did, or seek, however hopelessly, some form of regeneration? Mankind is not doing very well at the moment, but mankind has never done very well. Always expect the worst, and then you can never be depressed by your morning paper. As for action, note that history has a few lonely figures who did good or, fearing to do evil, did nothing. The impulses we share with the diabolic Marquis are best left to him, to be worked out in fantasy. We can never rid ourselves of these impulses by merely banning the books that most thoroughly express them. They are merely a spectacular symptom of one of the big human diseases. Whether the disease is curable is something we have still to find out.

Anthony Burgess is a devoted husband and affectionate father. His most recent novel is Enderby; *his latest contribution to* HORIZON *is "Johnson (?) on Johnson," which appeared in Autumn, 1968.*

The scene of the trial: a nobility-thronged Westminster Hall (see key opposite)

The most famous political trial of modern times opened in Westminster Hall, London, on February 13, 1788, between nine and ten o'clock in the morning, when evidence upon charges against Warren Hastings, former governor general of India, was taken before the House of Lords. So began the seven-year ordeal by oratory and public slander of Hastings, a man who, only a short time before, had held the fate of princes and dynasties in his hands.

The scene was as imposing as the twenty articles of charge of high crimes and misdemeanors against the eminent defendant. In the middle of the historic hall was placed a large table, at the head of which sat the Lord Chancellor surrounded by the judges, the masters in chancery, the clerks, and a number of law officers. On one side of the hall were placed the green benches of members of the House of Commons. Cloaked in ermine, the peers of the realm sat in the seats of honor. They, along with the lords spiritual of the Church of England, constituted the jury in this, the highest court that English law can convene, a court that had once sat in judgment on Lord Chancellor Francis Bacon and that had sent to the executioner the Earl of Strafford on the eve of the Civil War. Not for sixty-three years had this high court been assembled, and amid the great crowd jammed into the visitors' circle some of the great names of the day were to be seen: among them the actress Sarah Kemble Siddons, the historian Edward Gibbon, and the painter Sir Joshua Reynolds.

The proceedings formally began at twelve o'clock noon, when the managers of the prosecution entered. The diarist Fanny Burney, who had received her ticket from the queen, describes how "I shuddered, and drew involuntarily back, when, as the doors were flung open, I saw Mr. Burke, as Head of the Committee, make his solemn entry. He held a scroll in his hand, and walked alone, his brow knit with corroding care and deep laboring thought."

"How did I grieve," exclaims Miss Burney, "to behold him now, the cruel Prosecutor . . . of an injured and innocent man!" Edmund Burke was followed by an able and famous group of men. They included Charles James

By ALLAN NEVINS

THE TRIAL OF
WARREN HASTINGS

The defendant was the governor general of India
and the charge: crimes against humanity

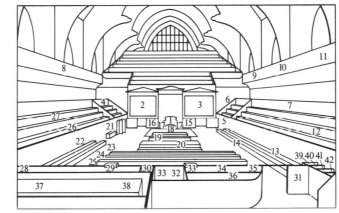

1 Throne
2 Queen's box
3 Prince of Wales's box
4 Foreign Ministers
5 1st Row, Duke of York's tickets
  2nd Row, Royal Household
  3rd Row, Lord Chancellor's tickets
6 Attendants on the Royal Family
7 Peers' tickets
8 Duke of Newcastle's gallery
9 Board of Works
10 Lord Chamberlain of the Household
11 Deputy Great Chamberlain's tickets
12 Peeresses and daughters
13 Marquesses
14 Dukes
15 Sir Isaac Heard, Knight Garter principal king of arms
16 Herald of arms
17 Peers Minor on each side of the throne

18 Judges seated on woolsacks
19 Lord Chancellor
20 Masters in chancery

21 Archbishops of Canterbury and York
22 Bishops
23 Earls

24 Viscounts
25 Barons
26 Speaker of the House of Commons
27 House of Commons
28 Managers and committee for the prosecution
29 Mr. Burke opening the charges
30 Shorthand writer for the Commons
31 Repeater of the evidence
32 Mr. Hastings
33 Prisoner's leading counsel
34 Counselors for the prisoner
35 Prisoner's shorthand writer
36 Counselors' clerks
37 Counselors for the managers and their clerks
38 Clerks of the India House
39 Shorthand writers for the Lords
40 Usher of the Black Rod
41 Deputy usher
42 Sergeant at arms and deputy

Fox, redoubtable leader of the Whigs, and Richard Brinsley Sheridan, dramatist and parliamentary orator. As the members of the House of Commons took their seats on their benches, the sergeant at arms rose and commanded silence in the court. A stentorian voice rang out: "Warren Hastings, Esquire, come forth! Answer to the charges brought against you; save your bail, or forfeit your recognizance!"

At this summons the small, frail figure of Hastings was brought to the bar of the House. The moment he emerged into full view he made a low bow to the Lord Chancellor and to the court; indeed, he bowed three times. "What an awful moment this for such a man!" writes Miss Burney, "—a man fallen from such height of power to a situa-

tion so humiliating—from the almost absolute command of so large a part of the Eastern World to be cast at the feet of his enemies, of the great tribunal of his country . . ."

It is not strange that so impressive an event created a sensation among the English-speaking peoples of the world and all admirers of British law. Nor is it strange that all subsequent impeachment trials, including that of President Andrew Johnson after the American Civil War, have followed the precedents of this great trial.

The impeachment of Warren Hastings was rendered the more memorable because it took place against the background of a chapter of Asiatic history full of color and melodramatic events. An old order was dying in India, and a

new one was being born. Just as the French revolutionists were soon to overthrow the *ancien régime* in France, so now a body of reformers were determined to destroy the prevailing system in India. Before the struggle ended, the old British Empire was brought under such heavy fire that its ultimate replacement by the British Commonwealth was plainly foreshadowed.

The trial was to center with cruel concentration upon Hastings, but the issues were more than merely personal. Thanks to the military genius of Robert Clive, and to the administrative talent of Hastings himself, the East India Company had recently established a dominion over India that no Asian power had been able to achieve. But the rule of the company was authori-

As governor general of India, Hastings stands with his wife and her Indian servant in a portrait completed in 1784, one year before his return to England.

tarian, and what was more disturbing, it was pervasively corrupt.

In the first half of the eighteenth century the agents of the East India Company had been traders, determined men who braved the heat, the disease, and the sodden monotony of India for only one reason: the hope of riches. The site of Calcutta, the headquarters of the company, was repellent. Built on an ill-drained swamp, it was full of cesspools and surrounded by a malaria-ridden jungle. Englishmen like Thackeray's Jos Sedley, who went out to make their fortunes, battled with clouds of flies and mosquitoes, with the sultry heat, and with diseases more deadly than tigers or cobras. Travel in Bengal was extremely dangerous. The roads were wretched, so that most communication was by river. The country was infested with bands of *dacoits* (robbers) and by wandering thugs—the word is of Indian origin—who were religious fanatics addicted to murder. Only the hope of wealth induced men to suffer such discomforts and perils. Kipling later summed up the special character of Calcutta in a line from his "Song of the Cities of India": "Death in my hands, but Gold!"

At that time, the men who sought their fortunes in Bengal were still only traders licensed by the nominal heads of India, the Mogul emperors at Delhi. When Clive and Hastings arrived on the scene, however, the Mogul Empire was rapidly breaking up, and both the French and the British saw an opportunity to take control. Two men of more divergent gifts and temperament it would be difficult to find. Clive was a man of action, dynamic and practical; Hastings was a man of thought, energetic enough, but scholarly in his tastes and philosophical in his outlook. Clive was the harsher of the two and was subject to fits of depression and gloom

(it was during one of these that he was eventually to take his own life). In 1756, when the nawab who controlled Bengal quarreled with the British, overwhelmed their forces in Calcutta, and shut his prisoners in the infamous "Black Hole," from which only a few escaped alive, Clive took masterful action. His little army of British troops and native allies overcame Mogul forces of twenty times their number at the battle of Plassey, and Bengal dropped like a ripe pear into his hands, a country as large as France and nearly as rich.

Virtually overnight the agents of the East India Company had become territorial magnates wielding political power. They were not slow to reap the advantages. Increasingly, in the years after Plassey, reports of bribery, extortion, and vicious crimes of every nature began to pour into England, and many Britons became convinced that the fair name of England was being sullied by company agents. The very term Anglo-Indian was becoming a byword for extortionate greed. The sight of a few fabulously wealthy Anglo-Indians, the famed "nabobs" of the day, seemed proof enough to many that the rumors and reports were true. As that sprightly observer, Horace Walpole, remarked at the time, "We are Spaniards in our lust for gold, and Dutch in our delicacy of obtaining it."

In truth, the whole structure of Indian government was wrong. It was

wrong that a set of merchants should hold imperial power. It was wrong that a company interested primarily in trade should enjoy such political authority. The revolt of the thirteen colonies made thinking Britons more sensitive to such considerations. Three and a half years before the trial of Hastings began, an India Act had been passed, putting the company partly under the control of the Crown and leading to Hastings's resignation as governor general. But the company agents were still the men on the scene, and they were several thousand miles from London in an age of sailing ships. To many reformers the Act itself was no guarantee of a change of spirit, nor did it establish the fundamental principle that it was wrong for one people to rule over another entirely in their own interest. This last was a new idea, and Edmund Burke was its champion. He intended, at this late juncture of his career, to drive this new conception home to the nation, and more importantly, to the agents of the East India Company serving abroad. The object lesson he chose for his educational task was Warren Hastings, and it was a savagely ironic choice, for Hastings believed as strongly as anyone that British rule in India must be equitable and fair.

Hastings had gone to India in 1750, at the age of seventeen, to serve in the lowly post of mercantile clerk in the East India Company at a yearly salary of £36. Ambitious, tactful, and patient, he had expected to rise step by step in the company hierarchy, earn the right to engage in trade for himself—the great perquisite of the company agent —and reap, in time, a well-earned fortune. He was only twenty-three when the victory at Plassey launched the East India Company into the deep and troubled waters of Indian politics. The situation was wholly new and called

The POLITICAL BANDITTI assailing the SAVIOUR of INDIA.

As a victim of persecution, Hastings fends off the attacks of a musket-wielding Burke, a thieving Lord North, and a black-jawed Fox in a cartoon of 1776.

for new talents. Hastings, a studious and quietly self-confident young man, possessed what was needed. A scholar among a band of narrow merchants, he taught himself Persian, the lingua franca of Mogul India. A keen observer—and respecter—of local laws and customs, he rose rapidly among men who looked with cold indifference on the "natives" who had so surprisingly come under their control.

In 1772, when Hastings was named governor general of India, he wielded more power over more people than any monarch in Europe. It was, however, a strange kind of monarchy, for the monarch, Hastings, was bound hand and foot by a single overriding requirement: he had to show a profit; for profit was what the managers of the company at India House in London ceaselessly demanded of him, regardless of wars, defense against invasion, or any other costs of governing. Hastings gave them their profit and simultaneously attempted to cleanse the system of its worst defects. It was Hastings who, almost single-handedly, laid the basis of just and responsible rule in India. He was a great man in a corrupt system, and he now faced a supreme test of his spiritual endurance; the most eloquent of adversaries were bent on portraying him as the wicked architect of the system itself.

The constellation of great names arrayed against Hastings at the trial requires some critical examination. By far the most illustrious figure was Edmund Burke. One of the greatest of British political philosophers, Burke gave unremitting support to the cause of freedom in Britain, the American Colonies, Ireland, and France. Although he never held a seat in any British ministry, he was one of the boldest and most powerful figures on the political scene. Beside him stood Charles

James Fox. Fox had brought into Parliament a daring but, in principle, sound measure for transferring virtually all the authority of the East India Company to the Crown. He had not been able to carry this, and he awaited new opportunities. He was a romantic figure, dashing and reckless, but he lacked balance. His private life was notoriously profligate, and he was known as one of the greatest gamblers of his time. He had drawn into Whig politics Richard Sheridan, who had followed his successful play *The Rivals*, with a still greater triumph, *The School for Scandal*. Sheridan had been elected to Parliament from Stafford in 1780. For his opposition to the American war, the Continental Congress had offered him a large gift, which he had refused.

But the management of the trial, and the driving force of the proceedings, were supplied by Burke. The "member for India," as his admirers called him, was a man of principle, filled with righteous indignation over the exploitation of the Indian people and conscious of the gross impropriety of entrusting the government of the great subcontinent to a chartered commercial company. Long before the trial Burke had denounced the company and decried its rule. Where, he had asked five years earlier, were the bridges and roads, the law courts and noble monuments, that even the cruelest of conquerors leave behind them? "Were

we to be driven out of India this day, nothing would remain to tell that it had been possessed during the inglorious period of our dominance, by anything better than the orang-u-tang or the tiger." But Burke's vivid imagination drove him, at times, beyond the limits of reason.

On the third day of the trial the prosecution began to introduce its charges against Hastings. In his opening speech Burke scaled the heights of interpretative eloquence:

I impeach Warren Hastings, Esquire, of high crimes and misdemeanors.

I impeach him in the name of the Commons of Great Britain in Parliament assembled, whose Parliamentary trust he has betrayed.

I impeach him in the name of all the Commons of Great Britain, whose national character he has dishonored.

I impeach him in the name of the people of India, whose laws, rights, and liberties he has subverted, whose properties he has destroyed, whose country he has laid waste and desolate.

I impeach him in the name of human nature itself, which he has cruelly outraged, injured, oppressed, in both sexes, in every age, rank, situation, and condition of life.

Hastings was accused of a vast catalogue of misdeeds: fraud, treachery, robbery, murder, "cruelties unheard of and devastations almost without a name." As Burke's magniloquent descriptions and thundering denunciations rolled across Westminster Hall, two things became apparent. The first was that Burke intended to try Hastings, not so much for any individual acts, but for what a later generation would call crimes against humanity: the ruin of the innocent, the turning of lands into deserts. Secondly, it was clear that the trial would not proceed very rapidly; Burke's opening speech, which was one of the greatest of his career, lasted four days, and there was

113

more, much more, to come.

It must have seemed then, even to an objective observer, that Hastings was guilty. To a man ignorant of the chaos and complexity, the intrigue and the dangers, that were normal conditions of Indian politics, the actions of Hastings might well have seemed as black as his accusers painted them. So it was with the first high crime with which Hastings was charged, and which Fox now described in a powerful speech of his own. It was alleged by the prosecution that Hastings had attempted, without right, and in a spirit of vengeance, to extort an enormous sum of money from the rajah of Benares, a demand that Hastings had backed up by trying to imprison the rajah and then violently suppressing an insurrection of his outraged people. The court was asked to behold a man so sunk in iniquity that he had shed the blood of a peaceful people so that India House might write its ledgers in black ink.

The second indictment for high crime proved even more sensational, and the hall was packed with an excited mass of spectators, for the glamourous Sheridan was scheduled to sum up the charge. The prosecution now alleged that Hastings had forced two hapless Indian princesses to transfer £1,200,000 worth of land and treasures to their worthless son and grandson, the vizier of Oudh, so that he could give it over to the company in payment of his debts. Two noble ladies set upon by a heartless rogue: Sheridan did not waste the opportunity for dramatics. Filial piety was his grand theme, filial piety and its ugly betrayal by a dissolute son in the grip of an evil corrupter, Warren Hastings, whom he pictured "now cringing on his prey, and fawning on his vengeance! now quickening the limpid pace of Craft, and forcing every stand that retiring nature can make in the heart! the attachments and the decorums of life! each emotion of tenderness and honor! and all the dis-

A melancholy Hastings, at seventy-eight, was portrayed by Thomas Lawrence in 1811, sixteen years after his acquittal.

tinctions of national characteristics! with a long catalogue of crimes and aggravations, beyond the reach of thought for human malignity to perpetrate, or human vengeance to punish!"

Turning the legal charge into a Shakespearean tragedy, Sheridan unfurled one of the greatest speeches in British history. Finished, he fell back into Burke's arms.

By now, more than a month had passed, and with several more charges to be read, it was obvious that at this rate the trial might take a decade to run its course. Besides, the court did not sit in continuous session. The peers of the realm, as Macaulay said in his famous essay on Hastings, did not intend to let jury duty interfere with partridge shooting, no matter how grave the case. Perhaps they were growing restive under the onslaught of invective poured out against the silent defendant, for it poured out with ever-increasing intensity. Again, Burke led the way. He intended to leave no room for mercy, not even the mercy of thinking that Hastings's crimes were, at least, imperial ones. They are, said Burke, "of the groveling kind, which do not usually grow upon a throne, but are hatched in dunghills." Hastings,

he said, had beggared the flower of Indian nobility to fatten the company's coffers, and his own. "He could not so much as dine without creating a famine." Day after day, month after month, the onslaught continued.

Hastings, meanwhile, labored without cessation to prepare arguments stating *his* side of the case. "My days pass in incessant writing and reading, and ever close with weariness," he wrote to his devoted wife, Marian. The Mogul crown prince was on his side. Most important of all, the officers of the East India Company stood with him. As more facts came to light, the black picture painted by Burke and his allies began to take on more suffused hues. The extortionate demands upon the rajah of Benares were seen to be in accord with Mogul law, a justified act of statecraft. The two princesses, pathetic victims of Hastings in Sheridan's great speech, turned out, of all things, to look upon their alleged tormentor as their friend. The complicated charges of robbery, bribery, selling offices, and so on all fell apart, as witnesses—even prosecution witnesses—came to Hastings's defense.

It was four years before Hastings finally had a chance to speak for himself. He spoke forthrightly of the conditions in India, of the harsh necessities of rule, of the progress he had made in government, of the prosperity that existed in the alleged "desert" of Bengal, and of the beggared nobles who yet looked upon him as an honored friend. As for the allegation that he made an illicit fortune, Hastings assured the court that had greed been his motive, he could have made, with his power, a hundred times the fortune in half the time that he served. "I gave you all, and you have rewarded me with confiscation, disgrace, and a life of impeachment."

As the case progressed, it became clear that his opponents were damaging themselves by their vitriolic intemperance. A reaction was setting in. By the middle of the trial Burke and the prosecution were looked upon by many as "political banditti" and the allegedly criminal Hastings as "the Savior of India." Indeed, the weight of evidence at the trial tended to prove that Warren Hastings had done great work in organizing and maintaining all that Clive had won in India. He had shown great ability and unconquerable courage. In effect, he had saved British supremacy in India by his swift and resourceful actions. The verdict of historians is that he should have been rewarded instead of being punished. In particular, historians have rejected as unsound the prejudiced and overrhetorical verdict of Macaulay in his essay on Hastings. This is also the opinion of an impartial American journalist and historian. "There is no department of government, of which he was not master," writes A. Mervyn Davies in his biography of Hastings. "The extent of his versatility, of his breadth of vision and manifold interests, is even better shown by what he did outside the scope of his ordinary duties than by what he did inside, remarkable as that was. He was, indeed, the ideal ruler, not content merely to administer and to govern but reaching out to the higher realms of the mind, working to extend the bounds of knowledge and improve the intangibles of civilization."

The outcome of the trial, which dragged on for another three years, could be predicted long before its end. Nearly everyone assumed that Hastings would be acquitted. The final scene came on April 23, 1795, before a great crowd. Hastings was ordered in and was then told to withdraw. Sixteen questions were put to each peer in turn, and each was asked to give his verdict of guilty or not guilty. Only twenty-nine peers in all appeared in their robes to give formal reply. The others, who had not attended regularly, were silent; they abstained from voting. On every charge the vote was heavily for acquittal—heavily but not unanimously, leaving just sufficient room for doubt to make the entire proceedings inconclusive.

The trial had cost Hastings several years of his life and a fortune in legal fees. It ruined forever any chance he might have had for a public life or for the peerage that he had once fully expected as his reward for service in India. He retired to the country, having reclaimed with what was left of his wealth the old family estate, Daylesford House in Worcestershire, where he lived until his death in 1818. As for India, the trial led to no new legislation. Two years after the verdict was passed, Edmund Burke himself was dead, though he had proved one point at the cruel expense of Hastings. The fate of the former governor general served notice to East India agents that England would no longer tolerate vice and corruption, even among the most powerful and most firmly entrenched.

The trial may have been inconclusive, but nonetheless men would remember it for years to come. They would recall Burke's extraordinary opening speech and recall how he and Fox and Sheridan had exhausted the rhetoric of invective in their savage pursuit of Warren Hastings. They might remember, too, Hastings's murmured denial, "It's a lie," as he sat hearing himself accused of the most infamous deeds. That murmured cry history would vindicate.

Allan Nevins, twice winner of a Pulitzer prize, is one of our most distinguished historians. Now retired from his chair at Columbia University, he is a senior research associate at the Huntington Library in San Marino, California.

STATEMENT OF OWNERSHIP, MANAGEMENT, AND CIRCULATION (Act of October 23, 1962; Section 4369, Title 39, U.S. Code)

1. Date of filing: October 1, 1968

2. Title of Publication: HORIZON

3. Frequency of Issue: quarterly

4. Location of known office of publication: 551 Fifth Ave., City, County, and State of New York, 10017

5. Location of the headquarters or general business offices of the publishers: 551 Fifth Ave., N.Y., N.Y., 10017

6. Names and Addresses of Publisher, Editor, and Managing Editor: Publisher, Paul Gottlieb, 551 Fifth Ave., N.Y., N.Y., 10017; Editor: Joseph J. Thorndike, 551 Fifth Ave., N.Y., N.Y., 10017; Managing Editor: Charles L. Mee, Jr., 551 Fifth Ave., N.Y., N.Y., 10017

7. Owner: American Heritage Publishing Co., Inc., 551 Fifth Ave., N.Y., N.Y., 10017. Names and addresses of stockholders owning or holding 1 per cent or more of total amount of stock of American Heritage Publishing Co., Inc.: American Association for State and Local History, Nashville, Tenn.; The Society of American Historians, Inc., c/o Prof. Eric F. Goldman, Dept. of History, Princeton University, Princeton, N.J.; Charles Bruce Catton, Irwin Glusker, Oliver O. Jensen, Richard M. Ketchum, James Parton, individually and as Trustee under Declarations of Trust for James Parton III, for Dana Parton, for Nike Parton, and for Agnes L. Parton and a Child of the Grantor; Joseph J. Thorndike, all of 551 Fifth Ave., N.Y., N.Y.; Virginia L. Thorndike, 520 E. 77th St., N.Y., N.Y.; Gerald P. Rosen, 3307 N.E. 16 St., Fort Lauderdale, Fla.; Merrill, Lynch, Pierce, Fenner & Smith, Inc.,* 70 Pine St., N.Y., N.Y.; Alexander Hehmeyer, 401 North Wabash Ave., Chicago, Ill.; Roger S. Phillips, P.O. Box 11, Rowayton, Conn.; Shearson Hammill & Co.,* 14 Wall St., N.Y., N.Y.; Barbara Joan Straus, c/o Irving Trust Co., 1 Wall St., N.Y., N.Y.; Alan Thorndike and John Thorndike, 11 Owenoke, Westport, Conn.; Evans & Co., Inc.,* 60 Wall St., N.Y., N.Y.; Clark Dodge & Co., Inc.,* 61 Wall St., N.Y., N.Y.; Gale & Co., c/o Harris Trust & Savings Bank, 111 West Monroe St., Chicago, Ill.

8. Known bondholders, mortgagees, and other security holders owning or holding 1 per cent or more of total amount of bonds, mortgages, or other securities: None.

9. For completion by nonprofit organizations authorized to mail at special rates (Section 132.122, Postal Manual): The purpose, function, and nonprofit status of this organization and the exempt status for Federal income tax purposes (check one)

☐ Have not changed during preceding 12 months
☐ Have changed during preceding 12 months

10. EXTENT AND NATURE OF CIRCULATION.

*Held for accounts of clients.

	Average No. Copies Each Issue During Preceding 12 Months	Actual No. Copies of Single Issue Published Nearest to Filing Date
A. Total No. Copies Printed (Net Press Run)	161,000	165,000
B. Paid Circulation		
1. Sales through dealers and carriers, street vendors, and counter sales	500	500
2. Mail Subscriptions	153,200	156,000
C. Total Paid Circulation	153,700	156,500
D. Free Distribution (including samples) by mail, carrier, or other means	3,200	3,000
E. Total Distribution (Sum of C and D)	156,900	159,500
F. Office Use, Leftover, Unaccounted, Spoiled After Printing	4,100	5,500
G. Total (Sum of E and F—should equal net press run shown in A)	161,000	165,000

I certify that the statements made by me above are correct and complete.

Paul Gottlieb
Publisher

tive was the culture of the Welsh. Even in the earliest examples there is nothing primitive. They were the product of an elaborate system of poetry making in which meters and themes were governed by strict bardic laws, and poets bequeathed their craft orally from generation to generation. The bards formed a guild, jealously protected, and they were important men at court; but though they wrote much honorific verse, singing the heroic praises of kings, often their work had a sidelong gnomic content that now seems to us very Welsh. Some of their poems were riddles, like this evocation of the wind:

> Without flesh, without blood,
> Without veins, without bone;
> Without head or foot; grown
> Nor more aged than young
> Than when first he forthsprung
> Into life, bold of breath.

Some were nature poems of the freshest and most direct kind, in which nature was not viewed allegorically, or even religiously, but was celebrated for itself—and sometimes even anathematized, like Dafydd ap Gwilym's fourteenth-century owl:

> She's a slut, two tuneless cries.
> Thick head, persistent crying,
> Broad forehead, berry-bellied,
> Staring old mouse-hunting hag.

And some were ecstatic poems of love or patriotism. In the thirteenth and fourteenth centuries the device called *cynghanedd* was evolved—a delicate system of alliteration that Gerard Manley Hopkins once defined as "the chiming of consonants" and that remains the hallmark of Welsh poetry to this day. All this was art of a rare sophistication: not designed for the common people, but specifically for the lettered and courtly upper crust, whose memories alone survive from that almost dreamlike era.

But through those years of feud, pride, and poetry, across the border to the east England had matured into a power of a very different style. Along the marches the Anglo-Nor-

man gentry mingled and often intermarried with the Welsh landowners. Elsewhere the two cultures remained irrevocably hostile, and the English and the Welsh were in a more or less constant state of war. There were periods of violent conflict and periods of suspicious peace, but always the presence of that formidable neighbor cast its shadow across Wales and sporadically united the Welsh princes in defiance. They fought to preserve their independence with every possible weapon: ambush, deceit, strategic retreat, diplomatic nicety. If the English often laid waste the Welsh countryside, the Welsh often left their hills to raid the rich English border towns. For two centuries after the Norman conquest the kings of England were seldom at peace with the Welsh. Some parts of the country they conquered or reduced to feudal dependency; others they never mastered.

The end came in 1282. Independent Wales was then united under a supreme prince, Llewelyn, who tried to make common cause with a group of English rebels. On his way to make contact with them, we are told, he was ambushed by a troop of horsemen, killed, and made a Welsh example: his head, ornamented with a crown of ivy, was paraded through the streets of London on the point of a spear and finally deposited on the topmost turret of the Tower of London, where it was left to rot.

He is known to Welsh history as Llewelyn the Last. The armies of Edward I marched into Wales and annexed the whole country to the English crown. The huge gray castles of the English arose, like magnificent warders, throughout the country of the Cymry; and in the most splendid of them all, Caernarvon, Edward's Queen Eleanor of Castile gave birth to a son. Tradition says that the king, in a gesture of historical ingratiation, ceremonially presented this first-born child to the Welsh people as their new Prince of Wales; and though this probably never happened at all, the English

remember it with a magnanimous glow and give the title to every royal heir, while the most intransigent of the Welsh continue to regard it as a crude imperialist ruse.

In Owen Glendower, for a few years at the start of the fifteenth century, the Welsh martial spirit flamed again. He was the last fighting champion of the Welsh, the last furious rebel to inspire his people against their English overlords, before they settled down to less violent methods of national survival. The English pursued him up and down the principality, but he eluded them year after year and infuriated them with ambushes, feints, and false alarms. He seemed to have supernatural qualities: the very elements were his allies, storms rising to his bidding and comets blazing in his honor. Shakespeare's Henry IV spoke for many an English soldier when he talked of ". . . that great magician, damn'd Glendower . . . as well have met the devil alone . . . for an enemy."

Glendower, supported at one time by a singularly inept French expeditionary force, fought the English with a mystical ruthlessness. Though a gentleman by birth and behavior, savage legends attended him. There is a story that he was once the guest of a traitorous kinsman at a country house near Dolgellau. While they were walking in the garden, his host drew a bow to shoot a deer, but suddenly turned and shot Glendower instead. The hero survived. The host was never seen again alive.

Owen himself never actually died, of course, though legend sometimes has him prosaically ending his days in his daughter's house in Herefordshire. In fact he simply disappeared into the Welsh mists, into some never-discovered stronghold, and waits there with Arthur, Merlin, the knights, and Guinevere until Wales needs him once again. He left behind him the castles of the English, some of the most terrible fortifications in Europe: tremendous on hilltops or at the sea's edge, battlemented and turreted all around, built generally by the labor of the conquered Welsh and garrisoned by English soldiers to whom the natives were barbarous savages with a tongue nobody understood.

All down the marches stood the fortresses, in those districts where the Welsh and English had cautiously intermingled, to protect the comfortable market towns of the border against the predatory hill people. Others commanded the ports or the crossroads, or merely stood as warnings in the countryside, their mailed sentries peering out through arrow slits upon the laboring peasantry below. English suspicion of the Welsh, which has never died, was born in the long years of conflict; the years of occupation coarsened it with a streak of contempt —or perhaps of bewilderment, because from that day to this the English have never quite understood what the Welsh are all about.

For some five centuries they did their baffled best to obliterate Welshness. Then, in 1485, Henry VII won the throne of England. He was a Welshman himself, the Tudors having sprung from the island of Anglesey off the northwest coast, and in some ways his kingship brought a new serenity to the Anglo-Welsh relationship: Welsh gentlemen occupied posts at court in London and moved more easily than ever before in English society. In other ways, though, the consequences were less happy, for the Welsh gentry brought back from their English excursions a growing taste for English ways and values.

Its native leadership aborted, Wales was deliberately integrated with its suzerain neighbor. In Wales as in Ireland, the English believed strongly in the value of assimilation, and thought that these uncouth hill people were really no more than primitive Englishmen only waiting to be enlightened. There was no religious conflict, for the Welsh had accepted the Reformation. Like the landowners, the bishops

and clergy became agents of Anglicization—they were often English themselves—and gradually, year by year, century by century, a clamp of Englishness was laid upon the principality. In 1536 Wales, already subject to the English crown, was formally made part of the realm by an Act of Union—the first step toward the creation of the United Kingdom and the beginning of the constitutional absorption of the little country.

Economically Wales became no more than an English appendage. Welsh wool went mostly to feed English looms, and the old Welsh cottage industries languished. Welsh livestock was driven in such a constant stream to the horse fairs of England that all over the southern English counties the highway inns knew their drovers— wild, queer men they must have seemed, with their broken English and their esoteric jokes, dressed in the coarse woolen cloaks of the mountains, often lapsing into their outlandish language or bursting into inexplicable ballads. Now all the main roads in Wales led to England, and when the railroads came they, too, seldom ran from south to north but across the grain of the mountains, connecting the ports and coal fields of Wales with their English markets.

Most resolutely of all did the English fall upon the Welsh language. They rightly saw its survival as a standing threat to their own supremacy, and they determined to expunge it from the Welsh memory. The Act of Union declared that "no person or persons that use the Welsh Speech or Language shall have or enjoy any Manner, Office, or Fees within this Realm of England, Wales, or other of the King's dominion, upon pain of forfeiting the same offices or Fees, unless he or they use and exercise the English speech or Language." Three centuries later the London *Times* was still calling the Welsh language "the curse of Wales," and Matthew Arnold could write, in his *Study of Celtic Literature:* "The sooner the Welsh lan-

guage disappears . . . the better; the better for England, the better for Wales itself."

The use of Welsh was forbidden in state schools and in official communications. Children who spoke it were sometimes to be seen with placards around their necks, saying "No English." The proportion of Welsh-speaking Welshmen diminished each year, as official disapproval had its effect and as the English culture spread into all but the remotest corners of Wales.

By the end of the nineteenth century Wales was hardly a nation any longer, except in a covert, spiritual sense. The southern counties were isolated from the north, and there was no capital. For a convenient place of national assembly the Welsh were forced to cross the border to English cities like Chester or Shrewsbury. Welsh seafarers looked to Liverpool as their home port. Welsh soldiers, who had been famous for centuries as archers and as mercenary captains all over Europe, now joined the colors in the Welch Regiment, the Royal Welch Fusiliers, or the South Wales Borderers. Able Welshmen in all the professions naturally gravitated across the border, where the opportunities were, and many of them reached the highest positions the state could offer. There were many Welshmen to agree with Matthew Arnold, that the survival of Welshness was only a drag upon the people, condemning them to provincial isolation and impotence.

Yet through it all the feeling of Welsh nationality never died. If most educated Welshmen seldom boasted of it, it lived on among the common people, who were less exposed to the blast of English example and less ambitious to become Her Majesty's Lieutenant-Governor in the Seychelles. In cottages and farmhouses the Welsh language was still cherished, in the way that defeated patriots elsewhere might prize a royal relic. The Bible, translated into Welsh in the sixteenth century, had been a shrine of the old language; and the Welsh Nonconformist revivals of the nineteenth century gave the people a new focus of national loyalty—a dour Calvinist focus, indeed, that did much to dampen their natural merriment and divide them from the Anglican Anglo-Welsh but did enable them to feel a separate people still, honoring their own values and singing their own lugubrious hymns.

All over the country the old ways, unpredictably and unobtrusively, survived. The bards and music makers with their harps still gathered at country eisteddfods, to express themselves in forms and rhythms altogether outside the English ken. The poachers irrepressibly looted the preserves of English or Anglo-Welsh landlords, abetted always by the general public and sometimes by police and gamekeepers as well. In 1860 the eisteddfod was revived as an annual national festival of art and patriotism, where never a word of English would be heard: a festival that was comic enough in its druidic trappings and trumped-up pageantries but very real in the emotions it inspired.

Most miraculously of all, there survived that inner germ of Welshness, that softness and sleight of hand that had been characteristic of this people always. Many Welshmen served the British crown in its boldest periods of imperialism, and the Welsh regiments figure in all the grandest annals of British arms. Yet there was often a gentle indirectness to the most Anglo- of Anglo-Welshmen that tempered their militance: it is easy to imagine that subject peoples of the old Empire felt Authority to be a little less aloof if there happened to be a Llewelyn, a Price, or a Griffith up at Government House. When the Egyptian Nationalist Arabi Pasha was imprisoned by the British in 1882, he found himself in the charge of an Arabic-speaking Welsh officer, Baldwin Evans of Rhuddlan. The boys at Eton unanimously voted that Arabi ought to be hanged for his patriotism, and Queen

Victoria herself privately agreed with them. Major Evans was apparently more placable, for a letter from captive to captor survives and seems to speak of the legendary Welsh courtesy of the heroic age, an age when prisoners of the Welsh were entertained with poetry and courtliness, in rush-lit mountain halls.

In the name of God, the Merciful and the Compassionate. My good and Honorable Friend, Mr. Evans.

I beg to offer you my devotion for the great zeal and trouble you have taken on our behalf during the examination of our case, and also for your frequent visits to us in our prison cell. I pray God to reward you for your great kindness to us in our hours of grief and darkness, and we beg of you to accept our most grateful thanks. I have done this in my own hand to be a remembrance and a lasting sign of the great esteem and friendship I have for you.

Ahmed Arabi, The Egyptian

*I*n 1890 a young man from the North Wales village of Llanystumdwy, within sight of Snowdon on the shores of Cardigan Bay, was elected Member of Parliament for Caernarvon and went off to London consumed with ambition. He was as fiery a newcomer as Westminster ever knew: a Welshman of the oratorical kind— passionate, arrogant, seductive to women and maddeningly fascinating to men—who could twist a crowd's emotions with an adjective or an inflection and gave an unforgettable impression of purposeful charm. Lloyd George went to Parliament as a Liberal; but above his head on election day, so he said, was the "Banner of Wales . . . borne aloft"—for his opponent was the rich Anglo-Welsh squire of his childhood village. Everybody knew that he stood first and last for Wales. He became one of the most celebrated and controversial of British prime ministers, but he was also the first statesman of a new Wales.

For the supreme anomaly of Welshness is that in our century it has been

getting Welsher. The triumphant career of Lloyd George gave Welsh patriotism a tremendous fillip, and he has been a national hero ever since, so that pilgrims still come to his grave beside the river Dwyfor. In the past thirty years, with the decline of the imperial ideal and the emancipation of Ireland, London has looked with a more tolerant eye upon the peculiarities of the Cymru. The various prohibitions on the Welsh language have been progressively relaxed; now, for example, a man may plead his case in Welsh in a law court, or apply for National Assistance in Welsh. Schools have become bilingual. There are radio and television programs in Welsh; indeed the BBC has become the most potent instrument of the Welsh culture, replacing the chapels as the chief patron of Welshness.

Welshness, once a condition many people were rather ashamed of, has become a cause for pride. The Welsh, hampered in the past by complexes of inferiority toward the English upper classes, now suddenly find themselves equals after all. That grandly imposing Empire, in which many Welshmen felt themselves to be conquered vassals, has sunk, with all its guns and trumpets, leaving the English themselves struggling to find a national purpose and maintain a national identity. The magnetism of a united Britain has lost much of its pull: if London is no longer to be a world center of enterprise, power, and excitement, Welshmen are beginning to say, then let us invest our energies at home. If that great Empire of the British is lost, then let us wave the red dragon at home.

Welsh nationalism is now a political force in the principality. It takes many forms—attractive, repulsive, noble, or nonsensical—according to one's point of view. Plaid Cymru, the Welsh Nationalist Party, has called for complete independence from the United Kingdom, with Welsh armed forces and Welsh ambassadors. In the meantime the party has already returned its first

In 1911 Edward, Prince of Wales, now the Duke of Windsor, is presented to the Welsh by King George V and Queen Mary.

Charles, the present Prince of Wales, whose investiture will take place in Wales this July, scans an antiroyalist poster in Cardiff.

member to Westminster, where he was effusively welcomed by all and especially by that astonishing proportion of M.P.'s of all parties who promptly declared themselves to be Welsh by origin. Welsh Liberals stand for less drastic reforms, and on one issue they probably command a majority of Welsh opinion: they want a Welsh Parliament with powers to control internal affairs, leaving matters of defense, foreign relations, and the higher economy to London.

But the exuberance of Welsh pride today has a dark side. Those long centuries of humiliation have not been universally forgiven, and there are extremists in Wales who are vindictively intolerant of anything English and would even use force to break away from the Crown. It is one thing for a municipality to augment its English street signs with parallel signs in Welsh; it is quite another to remove the English altogether, so that a substantial proportion of the citizenry cannot make head nor tail of them. Societies of bitter fanaticism are at work. In some schools teachers allow no English to be spoken, in or out of class, so that children go out into the world fluent in a language that is understood by only about a quarter of their Welsh fellow citizens and by al-

most nobody else at all. Chalked on railway bridges and mountainsides are the slogans of the Free Wales Army, a force apparently organized on Irish lines, whose members are sometimes to be heard of undergoing assault courses in lonely glades, or being guardedly interviewed on television. There have already been several cases of explosive sabotage, and caches of arms are not infrequently found.

How much this means, how menacing are what Kipling called, in an Irish context, "the secret half a country keeps, the whisper in the lanes," 1969 will probably tell us: for then the present Prince of Wales is to be formally invested at Caernarvon Castle —Prince Charles, that is, heir to the throne of the United Kingdom. It was at Caernarvon that the first of the Anglo-Welsh princes made his debut; there, too, in 1911, the young Duke of Windsor was presented to the Welsh with fanfares, panoplies, and David Lloyd George in the improbable capacity of Castle Constable. To most Welsh people this event will probably seem a harmless junket. To the hoteliers and tourist offices it will be a godsend. But to the extremists it will surely seem to be the very travesty of a royal occasion—the twenty-second in the line of alien princes,

foisted upon Wales in the supreme architectural embodiment of Welsh subjugation!

Then, perhaps, we shall see what the future of Wales is to be. Perhaps the Welsh really will call Glendower back and follow his dragon standards to lonely glory, isolated in their own traditions a very small nation re-establishing its nationhood in an age of superpowers and dissolving frontiers. Or perhaps they will follow a grander instinct, and generously developing in their own Welsh way, feeling themselves equal members of a much wider whole, make a richer contribution to the fascination and the gaiety of the nations than ever before. Whichever way they choose, we may be sure that the Welsh will never again relapse into the obscurity of a conquered people. As the allures of power, splendor, and size seem to weaken in the world, so the idiosyncracies of the Welsh, their gifts of lyrical ellipsis and side step, melody and gentle flourish, will find them ever more readily that perennial object of Welsh ambition—a large, attentive, and sympathetic audience.

Between jaunts to far-flung places James Morris lives near the small Welsh town of Criccieth on Cardigan Bay.

How to insult everyone regardless of race, color, creed, or national origin

There is a current variation of a military joke that may have had its counterpart in the Roman legions. A visiting Congressman asks a wounded American soldier in a base hospital in Vietnam how many VC he got before he was wounded. The soldier replies that he wasn't exactly fighting the Vietcong when it happened and explains that he had been taught to flush out Vietcong among the peasantry by saying "Ho Chi Minh dù me!" a scurrilous reference to Ho's parents that would enrage and penetrate the disguise of any true Vietcong. One day he tried it on a suspicious-looking peasant on the far side of a road who simply looked up and replied, "President Johnson dù me!" And, he explains, "as we were shaking hands in the middle of the road, we were both hit by a weapons carrier."

The world traveler finds that insults, while displaying a wide variety of imagery, tend to fall into three general classes. The first includes the multiple variants of "idiot," or "fool," and the second accuses the recipient of moral or physical degeneracy on the part of himself or his parents, usually his mother. The third, a simple insulting reference to the other person's nationality, religion, or color, can almost be predicted from the geographical position or national composition of the country or language in question. For example, call a Greek a Turk, or vice versa, and you have already insulted him magnificently. The Chinese can always insult a white man by referring to him as *yang kuei* ("foreign ghost," because of being so pale). However, this sort of slur should not be considered a true insult, since it cannot be used between people of the same nationality.

The traveler to France may easily recognize such standard insults as *imbécile*, *animal*, and even *crétin*. It is more serious to call someone a *vache* ("cow"), *chameau* ("camel"), *salaud* or *saleté*, these last two having the meaning of "dirt." For the sake of effect, all of these insults can be prefaced with *espèce de . . .* ("kind of". . .). French possesses also a frequent and unusual use of the "stupid" category of insult wherein the word *con* (the female organ) is used to describe a stupid or unlikable person. This

is often lengthened to *connard*, a word that is familiar to anyone who has driven a car in France and that is occasionally accompanied by the holding of the right index finger to the right temple and twisting it.

The supreme insult for a woman in Latin countries is the common term for "prostitute"—*putain* or *pute* in French, *puta* in Spanish and Portuguese, and *putana* in Italian. However, the subtle French have converted the regular word for "girl" or "daughter"—*fille*—into a like meaning. So, when in France, be especially careful how you use the word *fille*; the best plan is always to say "young girl"—*jeune fille*—rather than *fille* by itself.

Spanish goes one step farther, using *tu madre* ("your mother") so often as an insult that there is a tendency to avoid or disguise the term *madre* in polite conversation. Thus, if you wish to inquire about someone's mother, you may say *su señora madre* (literally, "your lady mother") or *su mamá* ("your mommy"). Of course it is all right to refer to your *own* mother, because everyone knows you would never insult *her*, motherhood still being very much "in" in the Spanish-speaking world. An even more violent insult is a two-syllable word (*chinga*) prefixed on *tu madre*, suggesting an illogical and improbable course of action, an expression so well known among speakers of Spanish that it can be whistled or even sounded out on an automobile horn in the rhythm: long, short, short, long, short.

In Germany the guttural force of the language tends to make the insult seem even nastier. What could sound worse than *verdammter Schweinehund* ("damned pig-dog")? *Schuft* is the equivalent of "jerk," and *Trottel* corresponds to "fool" or

"idiot," to be emphasized by banging on your right temple with your fist.

Russian contains an insult for a worthless drifter, *b'yezpasportnik* ("one without a passport"), since local passports have been required in Russia by both old and new regimes. A sort of elegant insult in modern Russia is *nyekulturniy* ("uncultured"). The older and more violent insults still exist, however; such as *durak* (the village idiot), *sukin sin* (bitch's son), *huy sobaki* (dog's member), and even *huy morzhevyi* (walrus's member).

When we come to Greece, we find an unusual gesture that has the force of the strongest spoken insult: holding your hand palm outward to the person you are insulting. This is called the *mountza* and usually provokes violence in the insultee, or perhaps a reply in the form of a double *mountza* —both palms, or striking the back of the right palm with the left as if to push the *mountza* even closer to your opponent. By an amazing linguistic coincidence, a recent American car was named the Monza—an interesting example of stacking the cards against a sales potential to Greeks.

In Moslem countries the most effective insults have to do with dogs. Dogs are generally in disrepute throughout the Moslem world because one of their number, about one thousand, three hundred and forty-two years ago, barked at and thereby caused the betrayal of Mohammed when he was hiding in a cave. Turks express this insult by saying *it* ("dog"), and the Arabs by *Ya, ibn kalb!* ("Oh, son of the dog!").

The favorite Chinese insult is *too-tze* ("turtle"), suspected by the Chinese of incestuous proclivities. Further, there is *tieu na ma*, which is similar to the standard Spanish insult about one's mother.

Insults may be interesting to consider and to compare, but not to use. The tourist or traveler should rather consider the Chinese proverb *fan she shih tzu erh ho shuo* —"turn tongue ten times, then speak."

Charles F. Berlitz, the grandson of the founder of the Berlitz language schools, is the author of 190 books and record courses on languages. He speaks thirty languages.

By CHARLES F. BERLITZ